ANNE BOLEYN.

ANNE BOLEYN:

A TRAGEDY.

BY

GEORGE H. BOKER,

Author of "Calaynos," &c.

PHILADELPHIA:

A. HART, LATE CAREY AND HART,

126 Chestnut Street.

1850.

PHILADELPHIA:
T. K. AND P. G. COLLINS, PRINTERS.

DRAMATIS PERSONÆ.

HENRY VIII,	*King of England.*
DUKE OF NORFOLK,	*Uncle to the Queen.*
DUKE OF SUFFOLK.	
DUKE OF RICHMOND,	*Natural son of the King.*
MARQUIS OF EXETER.	
EARL OF ARUNDEL.	
VISCOUNT ROCHFORD,	*Brother to the Queen.*
THOMAS WYATT.	
SIR HENRY NORRIS,	*Groom of the Chamber.*
SIR WILLIAM KINGSTON,	*Lieutenant of the Tower.*
MARK SMEATON,	*Groom of the Chamber.*
RALPH LONEY,	*A creature of Suffolk's.*
QUEEN ANNE,	*Formerly Anne Boleyn.*
JANE SEYMOUR,	*A Maid of Honour.*
MARY WYATT,	*A Maid of Honour, sister to Thomas Wyatt.*
VISCOUNTESS ROCHFORD,	*Sister-in-law to the Queen.*
LADY BOLEYN,	*Aunt to the Queen.*
MRS. COSYNS.	

Lords, Ladies, Knights, Ushers, three Informers, Officers, Heralds, Guards, Citizens, Attendants, &c.

SCENE, London and Greenwich.
Time, A. D. 1536.

PROLOGUE.

"Besotted dunce!" some modern Dennis cries,
And shakes his pen, and rolls his threatening eyes;
"Shalt thou, presumptuous bantling, dare to tread
The wondrous path where mighty Shakespeare led?
What, use his characters—re-write them too,
Changing the sterling old for feeble new!—
Perish, aspiring impudent!" and then
The foolscap quivers 'neath his fiery pen.
Hold, noble Critic!—"What, draw Norfolk!—zounds!"
And the poor Poet writhes with inky wounds.
Prithee, dear Critic!—"Nay, and Suffolk, sir!
Boy, give my ink a deeper, darker stir;
Rouse all the venom in its sleeping dregs."—
Alas! alas! "The coward miscreant begs,—
Begs me for mercy! Vengeance, death, I say!
Use bluff King Harry in his twaddling play,
Of Anne Boleyn take another view!—
There, print my 'Notice' in the next Review."
But, says the Poet, with an humble look,
Good Master Bilious, have you read my book?

"I read thy book? ha! ha! the fellow raves!"
Not praise, but justice 'tis the Author craves.
Pray, sir, skim o'er it, dipping here and there.
"Thy fustian, wretch! I'd see thee"—Hold, don't swear!
My readers will. "Thy readers? bless the zany!"
And if they read not—'sblood! I'll not have any!

ANNE BOLEYN.

ACT I.

SCENE I. *A Room in Whitehall Palace. Enter, as from the Council, Duke of* NORFOLK, *Duke of* SUFFOLK, *Duke of* RICHMOND, *Marquis of* EXETER, *and Earl of* ARUNDEL.

NORFOLK.

Nay, nay, my lords, affairs must not stand thus.
She is my kinswoman, and I confess,
If but on my estate her influence bore,
I would pass it by unchecked. No private griefs
Should wring a word from me, nor tutor me
To raise the hand that snaps a natural tie.
But see, my lords—

SUFFOLK.

'Ods blood! we have seen enough:

We have been open-eyed, your grace of Norfolk.
I trust we hold one mind?

ALL.

We do, we do.

SUFFOLK.

Why then, your grace, we have stared ourselves stone-blind,
Stared all our man to palsied impotence
At this she-basilisk. Some years ago,
From the mere dregs and offscourings of your house,
We saw this girl emerge, and step by step
Crawl slowly upward to the top of power—
Why she was queen before her crown was on—
Till now she threatens us from such a throne
Of downright rule as queen ne'er held before.
Nay, pucker not your brows, good duke of Richmond,
While conscience echoes what I bluntly speak:
Your royal father, more than any here,
Has felt her deadly witchcraft.

RICHMOND.

Fie, for shame!
I thought this meeting one of policy:
It never crossed me that five stalwart men

Had leagued their brains to gabble scandal thus
Of a poor queen, whose sole discovered crime—
Heaven send a rain of such bewildering sin—
Is too much beauty.

NORFOLK.

Therein lies her power.

RICHMOND.

Then we depute you, as her nearest kin,
To play Saint Dunstan to this fair Elgiva;
To rase her eyes out, sear her blushing skin,
Twist off her nose, and slit her pretty mouth;
But O, 'fore heaven! lay not your manhoods off,
And stand a-railing like a pack of drabs!

ARUNDEL.

Patience, your grace; let Suffolk have his say;
This was but prelude to the main affair.

RICHMOND.

Nay, if his song cannot out-go that pitch,
Henceforth I'll herd with women. Know, my lords,
To ease you of her beauty's deadly grief,
Her so-called strongest hold, my father's love,

Is wellnigh yielded to a nimble wight—
No higher than your arm, your grace of Suffolk—
Through herald words, and showers of gentle looks.
Therefore, I counsel we withdraw our powers
Of bearded men, nor strive to win by storm
That woman's citadel, our sovereign's heart.

SUFFOLK.

Your grace may flout and game at holy writ,
Or any solemn truth; nor stands a fact
Less in repute, because an empty jest
Has cracked thereon, and shown its hollowness.

RICHMOND.

I cry you mercy, lord of gravity!
Now wherefore meet we? Exeter, speak out.
You have not strayed away in idle words;
From which I argue you have kept to heart
This grave affair.

EXETER.

Thus is it then, my lords.
We all have sorrowing seen the growing power
Of her we call the queen—we call, I say;

For, in my humble judgment, Katharine,
Our sometime mistress—

RICHMOND.

Heaven defend us all!
He'll talk till cock-crow on that threadbare theme.
Will no one help us? Is there no one here
Who knows exactly why five fools have met?

NORFOLK.

Thus then, your grace. We peers have nigh become
A mere encumbrance in the council seats.—

RICHMOND.

Why here is a man who has his wits alive!

NORFOLK.

Spare me, your grace; too heavy this for sport.

RICHMOND.

Well, I'll be silent till the end. Go on.

NORFOLK.

This spawn of ours, whom I must blush to own—

RICHMOND.

Ha! more abuse!

NORFOLK.

—usurps the state entire;
Makes and breaks treaties; changes faiths and priests;
Empties the treasury, and fills it up,
By loans and taxes, such as she may will;
Sends one abroad, and calls another home;
Orders a marquis here, and there a duke.
All this she does, and more than I can name,
With but such counsel as her wits may lend,
Counting us peers as toys.

RICHMOND.

Ah, now indeed
We reach the body of things politic.
If 'tis a fight of wits, I am with you, sirs;
Though I misgive we shall be shrewdly cuffed.

SUFFOLK.

All this—your grace of Richmond, mark me well—
All this unqueenly power she strictly holds
By the fond tenure of our sovereign's love:
Let but the light, which now he suns her in,
Vanish in frowns, and this same haughty moon,
That floods our prospect with her filchéd beams,
Sinks to her native blackness.

RICHMOND.

So, stop there!
My lords, I'll join you in your enterprise
Against the sweet usurpings of our queen,
Perchance, when I behold you four tall men
Ranked on Tower Hill, the headsman standing by;
When meek-faced Suffolk is about to say,
"Good people, I confess I suffer justly."—

ARUNDEL.

Exeter, I have caught cold by standing here;
I feel the shrewdest of rheumatic pains
Twitching my spine above the shoulder blades.—
I must withdraw. (*Apart to* EXETER.)

EXETER.

Nay, nay, stand fast, he jests.

RICHMOND.

When noble Norfolk's humbly-worded letter,
"Touching his close connection with the queen,"
Meets in reply her gracious writ of death;
When scurvy poets sing in bastard rhymes,
"The doleful ballad of lord Arundel;"
When slip-shod wenches, with out-popping eyes,

And all unbreathed, pant out to passers by,
"Pray, tell me, sirs, where dies false Exeter?"
Then will I aid you, then I'll run amain,
Grovel and crawl, and kiss the royal shoe,
And howl for pardon which she will not grant.—
Till then, adieu!

NORFOLK.

Your grace will keep our counsel?

RICHMOND.

Zounds! I am a gentleman; and prove it, sir,
By having better business to my hands
Than the undoing of my female kin. [*Exit.*

EXETER.

He's a hot heart; but such are mostly true.

SUFFOLK.

What was the hint yon brain-struck bastard dropped
About the king's love suffering change to Anne?

ARUNDEL.

Nay, I know not; he dealt so much in tropes:
His grace of Norfolk is a poet's father,
He may resolve us.

NORFOLK.

I have thought of that.
'Twas a bare hint, but worth our scrutiny.

EXETER.

Ay, ay, indeed.

SUFFOLK.

I half believe it meant:
When Richmond bays, there is store of game afoot;
We have found it so.

NORFOLK.

I'll to his majesty.
If this prove true, our cause is wellnigh won.

SUFFOLK.

Your grace will summon us to hear the news?

NORFOLK.

Trust me; if true, I'll be too full to hold.

ARUNDEL.

Methinks the country air would ease these aches
About my neck, another talk like this
Nigh wrench my head off. (*Aside.*)

NORFOLK.

Till we meet, farewell!
Be secret, but be watchful.

EXETER.

Time is fate.

SUFFOLK.

We have not pulled the crafty Wolsey down,
To whimper tamely at a woman's heels! [*Exeunt.*

SCENE II.

Another Room in the Palace. Enter JANE SEYMOUR, *pursued by* KING HENRY.

KING HENRY.

Oh! prithee tarry! I am out of wind—
I'll not have breath to tell you how I love.
Stand, I adjure you, on your loyalty!

JANE SEYMOUR.

Now am I safe; I owe you loyalty,
And you owe me protection. (*Kneels.*)

KING HENRY.

Nonsense, child! (*Raises her.*)
You are far safer with plain Harry Tudor,
Than if the monarchs of all Christendom
Circled you round. For what are angry swords
To the raised finger of the baby Love?
I say, I love you; that implies respect.

JANE SEYMOUR.

Respect should teach you not to urge your love.

KING HENRY.

Sweetheart, pray hear me. I am all unused
To lovers' logic, to the mincing phrase
That snares a heart in nets of sophistry;
I'll not attack your passion through your brain;
But at your love's unconquered citadel
I'll sit me down, with rough, unmannered haste,
And bid you open in your sovereign's name.
Jane, do you love me?

JANE SEYMOUR.

With all duty, sir.

KING HENRY.

Tut, tut! no duty. Would you be my queen?

JANE SEYMOUR.

Your wife, my liege: the tempting name of queen
Makes no addition to a loving mind.
Love asks but love.

KING HENRY.

So, well said, mistress mine!
I never thought to win your dainty heart
By bartering for it an unfeeling crown.
Love comes unsought, nor heeds the voice of power:
The very gem which, from his purple throne,
A fuming king may gaze and thunder for,
Beneath the willows of some muddy brook
A listless rustic may disclose and wear.
Then, as mere Hal, the shepherd, if you list—
Barring all sovereignty with equal terms—
Say, do you love me? (*Kneels.*)

JANE SEYMOUR.

Maiden shame, my liege—

KING HENRY.

Liege me no more—Hal—Harry—what you will.

JANE SEYMOUR.

My maiden heart should send its blushing force

Of startled blood to whelm my guilty face,
While I stand parleying with her dearest foe;
Yet am I pale—ah! pale with fear, to think
What woful fate may be reserved for me,
If our right noble queen—

KING HENRY.

Hell blast the queen! (*Starts up.*)

JANE SEYMOUR.

Ha! did I gall you so? (*Aside.*) O pardon me!

KING HENRY.

Girl, I am wellnigh maddened by the queen.
A pack of yelling fancies bait my soul,
And each tongue seems to cheer the horrid rout,
When my fierce conscience cries—The queen, the queen!

JANE SEYMOUR.

O had I suffered her extremest rage,
Ere I had angered you!

KING HENRY.

Nay, I'll not scold.
Forgive me, sweetheart, my unmannered spleen.
My soul is much perplexed and tempest-tossed

About my marriage with this cunning queen:
I fear me, Lucifer made her a bait
To trap my soul.

JANE SEYMOUR.

O, you arch hypocrite! (*Aside.*)

KING HENRY.

Methinks the Pope was right—ay, must be right;
Since by the creed he is infallible.—

JANE SEYMOUR.

Not by the new one.

KING HENRY.

There the sorrow lies:
I have main doubts of our new-gendered creed.
If he be right, then is our union void;
For, by his voice, poor Katharine was my wife.—
I will consult my lords on this grave point.

JANE SEYMOUR.

Your nobles wear your eyes; but then the people—

KING HENRY.

I'll make half England see without their heads,

But I will wed you! Sweetheart, promise me,
If I can offer an unmortgaged hand,
That you will take it.

JANE SEYMOUR.

Thus I promise you. (*Gives her hand.*)

KING HENRY.

When next we meet, I'll show you many a way
To lead us from this labyrinth of doubt,
As soft and thornless to your pretty feet
As the rich velvet whereon you shall tread
To mount the dais of our English throne.
Till then, adieu!

(*They separate—she rushes back.*)

JANE SEYMOUR.

Sweet Harry, be not rash.

KING HENRY.

O, I would fawn, and play the stricken cur
To any groom, whose love-illumined wit
Could steal from time the weary chain of days
That links our purpose to its hopeful end.

[*Exeunt severally.*

SCENE III.

An ante-room in the Palace. Enter the Duke of NORFOLK, *meeting an Usher.*

NORFOLK.

Has the king risen?

USHER.

Anon, he will come forth.

NORFOLK.

I will await him.

USHER.

That is spared your grace.

Enter KING HENRY.

KING HENRY.

Ha! Norfolk, Norfolk, you have come in time;
There is no face more welcome than your own.
I would rather see you in this private way
Than in your dignity of counsellor.

NORFOLK.

Your majesty o'errates my little worth.

KING HENRY.

Not a whit, man. Sir Usher, keep the door;
Let no one enter till his grace withdraws. [*Exit* USHER.

NORFOLK.

I came on business of her majesty—

KING HENRY.

'Ods blood! the queen again! Enough, good Norfolk.
I have met no man, since I arose to-day,
Who came not whimpering of her majesty.
Pray change your style; the fashion had grown stale
Ere you were up.

NORFOLK.

Oh, ho! And how is this? (*Aside.*)

KING HENRY.

Norfolk, 'tis pitiful! No hour last night,
But my sharp senses, tuned to painful pitch,
Started, like guilt, upon the faintest sound;
The very mice stalked by like sentinels
Ringing in proof; the clock beside my bed

Hammered the hours like a gross forging smith;
The gentlest gust of air howled like the damned;
And when a noise, which in the joyous day
Would scarce make damsels wink, fell on mine ear,
Up from my restless bed, like one possessed,
I bounded, with wide-stretched and glaring eyes,
And half cried—Treason!

NORFOLK.

Sir, I am amazed.
Shall I go seek your majesty's physicians?

KING HENRY.

Ah! 'tis a grief their physic cannot touch.
My conscience, Norfolk.

NORFOLK.

Hum! join this to that,
And I might get some credit as a prophet. (*Aside.*)

KING HENRY.

My conscience—oh!

NORFOLK.

And 'twas his—"conscience, oh!"
Made such a pother ere Queen Katharine fell. (*Aside.*)

KING HENRY.

Nay; do you hear me? 'twas my conscience, sir.

NORFOLK.

Certes, within a month, another queen. (*Aside.*)
Grief has bereft me of the power of speech.
Might Cranmer help you?

KING HENRY.

No; you are the man.

NORFOLK.

Deign to unfold your majesty's distress;
And what so weak a man as Norfolk can,
He'll gladly undertake.

KING HENRY.

Hear, then, the cause.
You know our present queen—(*Listens.*)

NORFOLK.

And hear her, sir.

QUEEN ANNE. (*Without.*)

What, sir, deny me to his majesty?

USHER. (*Without.*)

But 'tis his majesty's direct command.

QUEEN ANNE. (*Without.*)

Stand from before me; I will answer it.

Enter QUEEN ANNE, *followed by the* USHER.

QUEEN ANNE.

Your highness—

KING HENRY.

Fellow with an usher's wand,
Hand me your cane. Begone, your place is wanted.

USHER.

Your highness, 'twas the queen—

KING HENRY.

Knave, bite your tongue,
Or you may talk your head off. Fly, I say!
And if within the precincts of our Court
Your traitor face is seen two hours from now,
I'll break your body in as many pieces
As this frail stick! (*Breaks up the wand.*)

[*Exit* USHER.

QUEEN ANNE.

Nay, royal sir, I pray
Some show of mercy to yon guiltless man.
If there was fault, believe it mine alone:
He dared not stop my entrance.

KING HENRY.

Say you so?
Well, madam, I believe it yours alone:
And much it vexes us that you, our queen,
Whose acts should but reflect our royal will,
Show thus a glass whence every traitor's eye
May take the foul impression of himself.

QUEEN ANNE.

My liege, forgive my over zealous haste;
The cause that brought me is no common one.
Our faithful Protestants in Germany
Are sorely pressed—

KING HENRY.

If they be pressed to death,
I care not. There are those within my realm,
Gross, headstrong Protestants, puffed up with pride,
Who should be sent abroad to get a squeeze.

NORFOLK.

Ha! ha! your majesty. (*Laughing.*)

QUEEN ANNE.

What owl is that
Crying so merrily as shadows thicken?
O, I beseech your majesty, sustain
The noble cause so happily begun!
You are the instrument, by Heaven picked out
From all the famous potentates of earth,
To work its high behest. Yea, after times
Shall lay your memory as a sacred thing
Upon their altars, radiant with such beams,
Shot clear from heaven, that slander's eagle eye,
Dazzled with light, can challenge no defect.
Most blessed of men! when the great trump of doom
Shall to its centre crack the startled world,
And cheek by cheek the king and slave awake,
Think what a band of heaven-persuading saints
Shall circle God, and raise their tongues for you!

KING HENRY.

Why here's Erasmus in a farthingale!
What say you, Norfolk?

NORFOLK.

Nothing now, my liege:
My brain is clearer in the council room.
I pray her majesty, the queen, may cease
To load her spirits with our state affairs:
The rugged shoulders of tried counsellors
Can scarce endure the burden of these times;
And much I fear—

QUEEN ANNE.

I see through what you mean,
Good uncle Norfolk. You are one of those
Big bloated toads that cumber up sweet earth,
A mere deformity in common sight;
Yet, 'neath the royal sun, you swell and swell,
Blinking your dull but self-sufficient eyes
Around the narrow bound your view may grasp,
And then shake heaven with angel merriment,
To hear you splutter—"Lord, all this is ours!"

KING HENRY.

'Ods wounds! forbear!

NORFOLK.

I'll give receipt for this. (*Aside.*)

KING HENRY.

Why rate you thus our friend and counsellor?
Your uncle, Norfolk, whose unfaltering zeal
Has seemed to be the shadow of our will!—

QUEEN ANNE.

But seen in sunshine.

KING HENRY.

If 'twould please your highness
To blow these noxious vapors from your mind,
Have pity on us, nor infect our ears.

QUEEN ANNE.

Your pardon, sir, if my unbroken tongue
For once ran riot with my better sense.

KING HENRY.

Ay, 'tis a wilful jade.

QUEEN ANNE.

But hear me out.

KING HENRY.

We'll make no purchase from the samples given—
Preaching and railing. 'Tis but courtesy,

If you require this room, that we withdraw.
Come, Norfolk, come.—What said his holiness?
[*Exit, leaning on* NORFOLK.

QUEEN ANNE.

What means this heavy feeling at my heart?
What means the king by this unwonted coldness?
What means my uncle by his insolence?
Why stood the king with an approving smile,
And heard my most unnatural enemy
Offer reproof in semblance of advice?
I have seen the time—ay, not a month ago—
When, in the fury of his lion mood,
He'd brained the scoffer with his royal hand.
But times have changed—ah! have they changed indeed?
Has my life passed the zenith of its glory?
Must I make ready for the gathering clouds
That dog the pathway of a setting sun?
Well, let them come! The blaze of my decline
Shall turn to gold the dull enshrouding mists,
And show the world a spectacle more grand
Than the young splendor in which first I rose.
Ha! ha! par Dieu! now this is marvellous!

A queen whose crown has scarcely ta'en the shape
Of her young brow, the anointing oil scarce dried,
The shouts still buzzing in my deafened ears,
With which the people hailed me on the throne;
Not two years queen, and moralizing thus,
Like fourscore crawling to its certain grave!
This is sheer weakness, the dull malady
Of little minds that chafe at little ills.
Great souls are cheerful with their inborn power,
Feeling themselves the rulers of events,
The sinewy smoothers of the roughest times,
And not the slaves of outward influence.
Despair is a fellow with a moody brow,
Who shuts a dungeon door upon himself,
And then groans at his bondage. Fear, avaunt!
Thy shades but trespass on my noon of power.

(*Several Courtiers cross the stage, bowing. Enter* THOMAS WYATT.)

Ho! Wyatt, hither.

WYATT.

Did your highness call?

QUEEN ANNE.

Where go you, sir?

WYATT.

I and these gentlemen,
Inflamed with holy zeal of selfishness,
Make to the Mecca of our hopes, the king,
A solemn pilgrimage.

QUEEN ANNE.

What news abroad?

WYATT.

Not a breath stirring.

QUEEN ANNE.

Say they aught of me?

WYATT.

If praise might tire the courtiers' flowing tongues,
Ere this they had been mute: to-day, as ever,
The sweets of Hybla drop from every mouth.
As I came here, a crowd of Protestants,
All fire-burned artisans and men of pith,
Their new-made zeal sitting like riot on them,

Brandished the fragments of some papal crosiers,
And cried—"Long live Saint Anne!"

QUEEN ANNE.

Mockery!
If history should hand my name to time,
God grant its fame may rest on firmer base
Than the disjointed sainthood of a mob!
I keep you waiting. Fortune speed your suit.

[*Exit* WYATT.

(*Another throng of Courtiers cross the stage, bowing profoundly.*)

These straws of courtiers watch the royal wind,
And first predict the coming hurricane;
Certes, as yet I see no adverse signs.
Some state affairs have galled the fretful edge
Of hasty Harry's rash but loving heart:
Anon he will return, and, cap in hand,
Cry, "Pardon, Anne!" But I'll pout and swell,
Tossing my head, and tapping thus my foot;
Then all my pride at one great, eager gulp
I'll seem to swallow, as I bound to him;
And then I'll pat his cheeks, and call him "Bear,"

And chide him gently for his angry mood.
But when his eyes blush at their starting tears,
I'll laugh aloud, and puzzle all his wits.
So from this egg, of seeming noxious wrath,
Shall spring a new-born love of double power.
To-morrow sees a messenger dispatched
To threaten Germany with fiery war,
If wrong befall our faithful Lutherans:
Whereat our uncle, the good duke of Norfolk,
Shall gnaw his nether lip off with chagrin.
Ho! cheer thee, Anne! darksome passages
Oft mount to prospects, but for them unknown! [*Exit.*

ACT II.

SCENE I. *A Room in Whitehall Palace.* *Enter* JANE SEYMOUR.

JANE SEYMOUR.

A queen, a queen! a real anointed queen,
With trains of maids and smiling courtiers,
Diamonds like stones, and softest velvet pall
To grace the shoulders of my majesty!
All eyes on me, my beauties sung in verse;
Each feature—ay, the tithe of any one—
More than enough to swell a rondeau up!
My wishes fairies, flying at a sign
To bring the substance of my latest thought!
My kin ennobled to the last degree;
My son a king, my daughters wed to kings;
My name the pith of gravest history!
This is too much! I cannot, if I would,
Put by the crown which fortune offers me.

But then the queen?—The queen o'erruns with pride;
Last Tuesday week she cruelly rated me.
What mercy showed she to poor Katharine?
I am but the instrument of justest Heaven
To make requital for her own misdeeds.
The king abhors her, and inclines to me—
Lo! nature points the path which I should take.
Just as I mount, so must the queen descend;
We hang in adverse scales. Now 'tis too late;
My faith is plighted to the king, and I
Will dare the issue for the glittering prize!

Enter KING HENRY.

KING HENRY.

All joy befall you, darling! (*Embraces her.*)

JANE SEYMOUR.

Welcome, sir!

KING HENRY.

Are you still constant?

JANE SEYMOUR.

Can you ask me that?
You have descended from your royal state,

And deigned to honor one so low as I;
Chosen me, unworthy, from the common throng,
Nor cast your eyes upon the maiden hands
Of princesses that wait outstretched for you:
As well might the poor clown reject the sun
That changes his grimed face to virgin gold,
As I refuse the glory of your love.
Henceforth my person is a sacred thing,
A common vessel turned to holy use;
And should you now disdain my little worth,
All your great kingdom holds no mate for me.

KING HENRY.

Tut! mistress, with your gloomy fantasies;
And be not jealous of my love so soon.
Ours is a mere exchange of heart for heart;
Crowns and such baubles enter not our trade.
That which I have, the sceptre of a king,
Possession makes nigh worthless in mine eyes;
That which I have not, your own beauteous self,
O'er all stale toys of royalty I prize.

JANE SEYMOUR.

Then be content; my heart is yours alone,

As virgin as the breast wherein it beats.
It rests with you to lift my fortunes up
On level with your own.

KING HENRY.

By Heaven, I will!—
But how, but how? Let us to counsel, love.

(Seats himself, with Jane Seymour *on his knee.)*

There's Norfolk, eager at our first design;
But he is a Papist; to restore the Pope
Part of his creed;—a doubtful counsellor.
If I retrieve the Pope's authority,
Upon the act my marriage is annulled,
And I am free. True, true; but pause we here:
How shall we satisfy the plundered monks
Whom we have ousted from their fat domains?
How our good nobles who possess them now?

JANE SEYMOUR.

And how the people?

KING HENRY.

Let them fight it out.
They are half and half, Papists and Protestants,

And so divided, easily subdued.
I mainly fear to reinstate the Pope;
His holy finger is in every dish:
I must be king within my own domain;
Yet if the thing must be—'Ods wounds! my love,
This matrimonial knot was hard to tie;
But 'twas mere pastime to undoing it.
Would that the Grecian's sword might cut it—Ha!—

JANE SEYMOUR.

What mean you, sir? Why do you glare around?
And pale as death!

KING HENRY.

As death!

JANE SEYMOUR.

Ay, and as fearful.
Rouse, rouse, sir! You are ill—I'll call relief.

KING HENRY.

Nay, sit you down again.

JANE SEYMOUR.

But are you well?

KING HENRY.

'Twas but a passing thought that tortured me,
Like one may feel who murders. Clasp me tight;
Pain would be comfort to such awful visions.

Enter QUEEN ANNE, *behind.*

QUEEN ANNE.

Ha!

JANE SEYMOUR.

O, good heavens! the queen!

QUEEN ANNE.

In luckless time
For you, base minion, treble traitoress,
False to yourself, false to your state and me!
The foulest sin that woman may commit,
Made doubly hideous by the circumstance!
What! in the palace that contains your queen,
The very seat of England's dignity,
Whence virtue, as the simple commons deem,
Springs to illumine this majestic realm!
Have you no shame? Wear you that brazen front
When I hold up a mirror to your crime?

Is not your Gorgon nature turned to stone,
At the bare glimpse of your own ugliness?

KING HENRY.

Peace, sweetheart, peace; all shall be well for you;
Your maid is guiltless.

QUEEN ANNE.

Have you found a tongue?
What sorcery bestowed this power of speech?
Or has poor shame, bedazzled at her glory,
Shrunk from the world?

KING HENRY.

This foully slandered maid
Is half distraught at your mad violence.

QUEEN ANNE.

And dare you, sir, before your injured queen—
You, the copartner of her guilt and shame,
Protect yon wanton?

KING HENRY.

Dare I, dare I, madam!
'Ods wounds! who's king in England? Hold your tongue,

You rank defier of your sovereign's power!
Have you not learned whose presence you are in?
Or must I teach you by some sterner means?

QUEEN ANNE.

Oh! shameless husband!

KING HENRY.

She is pure, I say:
And, by high Heaven, as pure shall you remain
From touch of mine, till malice gnaw you up!—
This is forever. Come, sweet mistress Jane.
[*Exit, leading off* JANE SEYMOUR.

QUEEN ANNE.

Oh God! oh God!—The king—Nay, Harry, Harry,
Come back; I will—Oh! killing agony!
Is there no pity in the heart of man?
Plead for me, girl—he loves you—plead for me!
I am his wife, your queen, your loving mistress.
I will forgive you, I will cherish you,
I'll love you dearer than my dearest friend.—
Gone, gone forever! Said he not, forever?
Kind Heaven, have mercy on my feebleness!

If this is trial of my strength, I yield;
I do confess my utter helplessness;
I bow me prostrate, a poor nerveless woman—
A queen no more. I'll trample on my pride,
And follow meekly where thy finger points.
By Heaven, not so! This is a grievous wrong,
By man inflicted. Devils ordered this,
And they shall pay it!—Hear me, writhing souls,
That minister around sin's ebon throne!
If to these murderers of my heart's dear peace
A child be born, may she, in that sweet time
When infant babble opes all heaven to her,
Feel the cold hand of death draw day by day
The clinging spirit from her! May her child
Live in the vexings of a troubled time,
And issueless die young! May he—O God,
I cannot bid a curse light on the head
Of him my child calls father! Bless him, Heaven!
Give him the peace which he has stolen from me!

[*Exit.*

SCENE II.

A Street in London. Enter MARK SMEATON *and* RALPH LONEY, *meeting.*

LONEY.

Mark Smeaton, if I breathe!

SMEATON.

Who are you, fellow,
That thus accost her majesty's chief groom?

LONEY.

So soon forgotten! Know you not Ralph Loney,
Whilom your school-mate? Shame upon you, Mark!
Had I turned Peter, and denied you thus,
When the big smith made at you with his hammer,
You had not borne your silken coat to-day.

SMEATON.

Ralph Coney—Coney?—

LONEY.

Loney, Master Mark.
How should I call your name, not knowing you?

SMEATON.

Think you, this is the first or hundredth time
That knaves have claimed acquaintance with my name?
We of the Court are known to every one;
And I in chief, as the queen's favored groom—
Nay, I may say, her most familiar groom,
Ranked more as friend than courtly servitor—
Am most conspicuous to the vulgar gaze.
It would but prove a new-come clown in town,
Had you not known me.

LONEY.

Here are tidings gained
To please his grace of Suffolk. This same Mark
Is worth my powder. (*Aside.*)—Bless me, gracious sir!
I pray forgive my vulgar forwardness;
Indeed I knew not of your dignity.
Your worship would not harm a thoughtless man.
Nay, frown not, good Sir Mark.—Do I misjudge,
In calling you Sir Mark?

SMEATON.

On the way thither;
To-morrow, or next day, that style may suit;
Perchance, a higher one. Resume your beaver.
Let me see—Loney—Ralph?—Upon my life,
When I reflect, I have a faint idea
That once I knew you.

LONEY.

I will freshen you.
Do you remember, on an Easter day,
How the fierce urchins, half insane for meat,
And rancorous with the bile of fishy Lent,
Into a green and filthy pool bobbed you,
Merely because they could? How I alone,
In pity of your plight—your slimy plight—
Your most nose-wrenching plight—

SMEATON.

Good Loney, cease!
The zenith-topping sun forgets the clouds
Which, in the dirty dawn, he struggled through!

LONEY.

Now what bystander that had seen you rise

From that green pond, fresh with your miry coat,
Had ever prophesied these gilded clothes?
And who that saw me, with my broken staff,
Thrash to their doors your routed enemies,
Could have foretold my present mean estate?
I should be captain of a great armada,
You should be dragging horse-ponds.

SMEATON.

Prithee, cease!
These boyish pranks disgust my nicer sense.

LONEY.

I would not vex you; but it comforts me,
And reconciles me to my lot on earth,
To summon back my childhood. As I then
Had my full hours of triumph and renown,
So have you now; thus fate is justified.

SMEATON.

You seem to be an honest fellow, Ralph;
Nor care I if from my abounding store,
Ever replenished by my gracious mistress,
I give a parcel. (*Gives a purse.*)

LONEY.

Luck be with you, sir!

SMEATON.

When that is emptied, I'll replenish it,
If you will drink my royal lady's health.

LONEY.

You stand high in her favor.

SMEATON.

Did you know
The height I stand, it would amaze your ears.
Adieu! we'll meet again. [*Exit.*

LONEY.

Farewell, poor fool!
We'll meet too soon for you. Hell snatch the purse!

(*Throws it from him.*)

It burns like heated brass. Now to the duke.
Mark Smeaton's vanity, a seeming trifle,
May in his grace's hands work great results;
Ay, even the unqueening of a queen.
Alas! alas! poor Mark, that thy fine feathers

Should draw the fowler's closely prying eye!
So must it be; why should I hesitate?
Curse on his bounty! While we are beasts of prey,
The little game must ever feed the great. [*Exit.*

SCENE III.

A Room in the Palace of the Duke of SUFFOLK. *Enter Duke of* NORFOLK, *Duke of* SUFFOLK, *and Marquis of* EXETER.

SUFFOLK.

Where's Arundel, Lord Exeter?

EXETER.

Poor man!
His over boldness in once joining us
Has scared him from a second wish of it:
One valiant thought has terrified the rest.
He bade me mention that some strict affairs
Drew him away. When we have won the game,
I pledge my faith, we'll have him bickering hot,
And bold as Mars to share the dangerous spoils.

NORFOLK.

We can well spare him. Since his majesty
Has shown such favor to our enterprise,
They who at first turned from us, virtue-sick,
Deem it a blessèd thing to be enrolled.

Enter Earl of ARUNDEL.

Welcome, my lord!

ARUNDEL.

A dear salute to me.
I rode four horses dead, to keep my faith,
And only reached you as the fifth fell lame.
Good Lord! good Lord! they say his majesty—
I had this from a sure but private source—
Has gained intelligence of our design,
And smiles at it. Ugh! sirs, I'm out of breath:
When I have blown awhile, I'll tell you more.

SUFFOLK.

Nay, spare your wind.

NORFOLK.

Poh! poh! don't anger him.
(*Apart to* SUFFOLK.)

ARUNDEL.

Ha! you know all?

NORFOLK.

Yes, every tittle of it.

ARUNDEL.

Then, sirs, to counsel.

EXETER.

Now he is head assassin. (*Aside.*)

NORFOLK.

His majesty is much perplexed with doubts;
Nor knows he, better than ourselves, a plan
To rid the state of his ambitious queen.
She has committed no so gross excess
As may subject her to the common law:
A faithful wife, untainted in her fame—

EXETER.

And so was Katharine.

SUFFOLK.

Come, come, be blunt:
We must destroy her, by fair means or foul.

Enter a SERVANT.

SERVANT.

Your grace's servant, Master Loney, waits.

SUFFOLK.

Let him wait, fellow—I am much engaged.

SERVANT.

I told him so. He said his business was
About the matter you have now in hand.

SUFFOLK.

Ha! said he so? Admit him then. [*Exit* SERVANT.] My lords,
Be not provoked by his familiar bearing.
He is my jackal, a most useful one,
But one who hates his trade.

Enter RALPH LONEY.

LONEY.

My speech is short.
I met a youthful schoolfellow of mine,
A rare musician, now her highness' groom:
The man 's a fool, and boasted of the love
His mistress bore him. He would go still further,

To gratify his itching vanity,
And criminate the queen.

SUFFOLK.

Go make him drunk;
Take witnesses, fit men, and pump him dry.

LONEY.

I will obey, sir.—'Tis but one man more. [*Exit.*

SUFFOLK.

You'll scarce believe, at times that fellow laughs;
But never when about my secret work;
Then he is ever sullen.

ARUNDEL.

A strange knave.

SUFFOLK.

But faithful.

EXETER.

Something grave may come of this.

SUFFOLK.

Ay, something which, by us interpreted,
May compromise the virtue of the queen.

NORFOLK.

Perhaps. O find me but some little charge,
Less weighty than the air-drawn gossamer—
Some dim tradition, gathered in a dream
Seen by the blearing vision of a drunkard—
Some hearsay mumbled by a maniac's lips,
With fever scorched upon his dying bed—
Some words the roaring tongues of angry blasts,
Or zephyrs, lisping through the sluggish trees,
Hummed in the ears of musing fantasy—
Find one of these, to frame a charge upon,
And I will warrant trial expedite,
And sure conviction, though an angel plead.

SUFFOLK.

I'll answer, Loney's craft unearths a charge
As horrible as death.

EXETER.

What mean you, sirs,
To bring a deadly fault against the guiltless?

ARUNDEL.

Ay, prove it too.

EXETER.

This is flat villany!
'Tis now too late to shape my course anew;
And England's weal outweighs a woman's life. (*Aside.*)

NORFOLK.

Should this affair fulfil its promises,
We'll meet anon.

ARUNDEL.

If 'twould assist you, sirs,
Pray use my house.

EXETER.

This fellow glows with zeal;
He'd stab she-Cæsar in the Capitol.
What is so cruel as cowardice in power! (*Aside.*)

[*Exeunt severally.*

SCENE IV.

A by-street in London. Knots of vagabonds occasionally cross the scene. Enter Viscount ROCHFORD *and* THOMAS WYATT.

ROCHFORD.

Here is indeed a walk to take a friend,
Good master Poet! Pray what place is this?
Are we in London or in Tartarus?
For, by my life, the visions we have passed
Seemed fit induction to the place of shades.

WYATT.

No, Heaven be praised, we are in "Safety," sir;
So call the thieves this well of girding walls.
Here is a place as innocent of rule
As the dun sands of savage Araby;
Here pilferers divide their filchêd rags,
And bolder robbers share their golden spoils;
Here crime is native, natural, unabashed,

Walking abroad in easy confidence;
Here treason stalks, the dreaded ghost of courts,
Whetting his knife, and mixing deadly bowls.
From yonder porch, I heard a hoarse-voiced Jew
Harangue a crowd of frowning murderers,
Cursing the king, the state, the holy church,
Until he choked with mere malignity.
On yonder steps, I saw a quiet wretch
Coolly thrust in an ell or so of steel
Between his brother's ribs.—There they both walk,
The Jew and murderer. No law is here,
Save what the dwellers make, and that is shifting.
I oft have thought the watchful eye of God
Upon this place ne'er rested; or that hell
Had raised so black a smoke of densest sin,
That the All-Beautiful, appalled, shrunk back
From its fierce ugliness. I tell you, friend,
When the great treason, which shall surely come
To burst in shards law-bound society,
Gives the first shudder, ere it grinds to dust
Thrones, ranks, and fortunes, and most cunning laws—
When the great temple of our social state
Staggers, and throbs, and totters back to chaos—

Let men look here, here in this fiery mass
Of agéd crime and primal ignorance,
For the hot heart of all the mystery!—
Here, on this howling sea, let fall the scourge,
Or pour the oil of mercy!

ROCHFORD.

Pour the oil,—
In God's name, pour the blessed oil! The scourge,
Bloody and fierce, has fallen for ages past
Upon the foreward crests within its reach;
Yet made no more impression on the mass
Than Persia's whips upon the Hellespont.

WYATT.

'Twas not to harrow up your heart with crime—
Though, haply, such amazement is not lost—
I brought you hither. 'Twas to stand beyond
The utmost pale and influence of the Court,
Where men interpret a malignant mind
From every look the changing features wear;
Find danger in the meeting of two friends;
Rank treason in devices of our arms;
Open rebellion to their gracious king,

Should we but furbish our time-rusted blades.—
Now, Rochford, listen.

ROCHFORD.

Heavens! you frighten me.

WYATT.

No, I but caution you. My tale, though sad,
May rest on fears as thin as summer clouds.

ROCHFORD.

Why that is cheering.

WYATT.

'Tis not for yourself,
But for her sacred majesty, the queen,
I have these vague misgivings.

ROCHFORD.

What, the queen!
Pshaw! Wyatt, was there ever woman blessed
As she is? Courted and bepraised by all,
Sharing no empty title in the crown,
No mere producer of a royal brood;
But by the force of her own intellect,

To all effects, an equal with the king.
Why, man, just now she stands at zenith height,
Flooding our land with peerless majesty,
The gaze and wonder of all Christendom.
The great reformer, Anne, pre-ordained
By Heaven to work its solemn purposes!—
Poh! this is idle—we are wasting time:
Your fears indeed were thin as summer clouds.

WYATT.

Ah! know you not, when the rejoicing sun
Has reached its mid-day station in the sky,
At that same time its mournful fall begins?

ROCHFORD.

Sir Poet, I confess me figure-beaten:
Now croak away.

WYATT.

What I shall tell,
My sister Mary told to me alone.
She says, of late her majesty remains,
Hour after hour, with dull and vacant eyes,
Picking the fringe around her garment's hem.

Anon, big tears, like slow-paced mourners, come
Forth from the woful mansion of her grief,
As if they followed at hope's funeral.
If they arouse her from this lethargy,
She looks bewildered, asks the time of day,
Appears surprised at lateness of the hour,
Gives more commands than she has several hairs;
Talking, meanwhile, at such a rattling pace,
In bitter sneers and heartless gayety,
That not an ear can gather her discourse:
And then again, all suddenly, she falls
Into her former state of revery.

ROCHFORD.

Good sir, you startle me. Art sure of this?
For 'tis the dreamy torpor of the brain
That oft foreshadows madness.

WYATT.

Very sure;
But 'tis not madness. Listen, till the end.
One day my sister entered suddenly,
But unperceived, the chamber of her highness.
Scarce had she crossed the threshold ere she saw,

Rolled in a heap and crammed into a corner,
The person of the queen. She stood amazed,
Not daring to approach; and saw such grief,
So absolute, so past all earthly bounds,
So fiercely raging to pain's topmost pitch,
That she shrunk quivering to the ante-room.
But there her ears made pictures to her eyes:
Anon, she heard her clawing at the floor,
Sobbing and railing like a soul possessed:
Then into one long, piercing, hellish scream
Of hideous laughter broke her aching soul.
At that my sister fled, with echoing laugh,
And knew no more till from a lengthened swoon
Her maids awoke her.

ROCHFORD.

This is past belief.
Without a doubt, the queen or she is mad.

WYATT.

My sister says, the king and queen ne'er meet;
That notes unnumbered of her majesty's
He has returned unopened. More, 'tis noised,
The king and Seymour's daughter oft of late

Have been observed together; that the foes,
Once secret, but now open, of the queen
Stand in high favor with his majesty,
And share his private counsels.

ROCHFORD.

Gracious Heaven!
If this be certain, there is more in it
Than I dare utter. Have I been bewitched,
That I remained o'erconfident so long?
Now you have mentioned it, a thousand things
Which I have seen, but shuffled by unweighed,
Rise to confirm the gloomiest belief.
My cold receptions, Suffolk's insolence,
Arundel's vaporings, Norfolk's tart replies,
My sudden dearth of courtly sycophants,
And Wyatt's warming friendship. Noble man,
Through all my life I never aided you—

WYATT.

Because I never asked it. Pshaw! George Boleyn,
Were we not playfellows 'neath Blickling's oaks,
Where first my muse essayed her feeble lisp?
Did you not praise and wonder at my rhymes,

And cheer my heart with kindred sympathy?
Have we not written sonnets and rondeaux,
In kindly rivalry, to Anne's eyes?
Did you not always swear my songs the best,
Ere half were read, and force fair Anne's hand
To place the laurel on my victor brow?
Can I forget you? Can I cease to see,
In England's queen, our little playfellow?
Forgive me, Rochford; this is not a time
To babble of our childhood. You are hemmed
With scores of bold and ruthless enemies;
And, God assoil him! the worst foe of all
Is the first man in England's wide domain!

ROCHFORD.

What shall be done?

WYATT.

Fly to her majesty;
Drain to the dregs her secret cause of grief;
Learn all her fears, the blackest of her fears,
Nor care to know her dimmest gleam of hope.
Armed for the worst, we gain a double strength—
The power to conquer at the last extreme,

And chance that such extreme may ne'er arrive.
I will not slumber. What the brain of man
Can summon from its viewless armory,
Shall be arrayed to battle for her right.
I'll see you safe beyond this wretched place,
And then we part, but not without a hope. [*Exeunt.*

ACT III.

SCENE I. *A Tavern.* MARK SMEATON, *drunk, with* RALPH LONEY *and three Informers seated at a table spread with wine, &c.*

SMEATON.

Now that's a song, and that's what I call singing.
Roar it again, brave master bull-throat, roar!

FIRST INFORMER. (*Sings.*)

Old sack, old sack,
Thou hast a happy knack,
When fortune deals a sorry thwack,
When friends may flout, and credit crack,
Old sack, old sack.

Old sack, old sack,
We'll bide the world's attack,
Though rosy Cupid turn his back,
We ask but this, that thou'lt not lack,
Old sack, old sack.

SMEATON.

Is that the end of your rare melody?
Loney, my boy—Loney, you are dull as mud—
Were you not ravished by yon fellow's song?
That is the neat's-tongue of true poesy:
Nature applauds it in the thirst it brings.
The song is a miracle; that one being full
Yet asks for more upon it. Wine, there, wine!

(*They drink.*)

What are such poets as my lord of Surrey,
Or whining Wyatt—Some one curse Tom Wyatt.
You singer with the stormy lungs, pray curse
This Thomas Wyatt! Have I ne'er a friend
Whose oaths are potent? Curse him black and blue,
My rival Wyatt!

LONEY.

Rival, boy! and how?

SMEATON.

Who is my love? Answer me, leather-lungs.

FIRST INFORMER.

Nay, sir, I know not.

SMEATON.

Then you are an ass,
Not knowing, and a wizard, knowing her.

LONEY.

We cannot miss by drinking her a round.
Give us the toast.

SMEATON.

Here's to our noble queen! (*Drinks.*)

LONEY.

That's good and loyal, and we'll quaff it off;
But not what we intended. We would drink
To your sweet darling, to your pretty May,
Your wanton plaything. Come, boy, never halt!

SMEATON.

Loney, observe me—every piece of me—
Edgewise, before, behind. Now tell me, sir,
What woman in this realm is worthy of me?

LONEY.

Some great one, without doubt.

SMEATON.

I say, the queen.

LONEY.

Now mark him, sirs. (*Apart to the* INFORMERS.)

INFORMERS.

Ho! ho! the man is drunk!

SMEATON.

What do you take me for, you foul-mouthed knaves,
A man of worship, or a common liar?
Where have you lived, you scum of filthy earth,
Not to know me?

LONEY.

Pardon the simple men;
Indeed they knew not of your dignity.
This is her majesty's chief groom of state—
The very front door to her royal ear;
You must needs pass him ere you reach the queen—
Pray you, respect him.

FIRST INFORMER.

O, that alters it;
A royal servant.

SMEATON.

Are the villains blind?
Well, well, I have comfort.

LONEY.

What may comfort you?

SMEATON.

That some fair day a goodly son of mine
May mount the throne, and chop off all their heads.

LONEY.

Mark that again. (*Apart to the* INFORMERS.)

SECOND INFORMER.

There is not a word escapes:
I have engrossed it in my table-book.

SMEATON.

Come, Loney, come; we'll leave these stupid knaves.

SECOND INFORMER.

Whither away, sir?

SMEATON.

To the queen, good dolt! (*Going.*)

LONEY.

Forget not, masters, "To the queen," he said;
And at this hour. So, boy, away, away!
[*Exit with* SMEATON.

SECOND INFORMER.

There is hanging in this.

THIRD INFORMER.

Curse him! what care I?
I nigh had struck the braggart down myself,
For slandering thus her gracious majesty.
The base, ungrateful cur! I'll see him hang. [*Exeunt.*

SCENE II.

The Queen's Apartments in Whitehall Palace. Enter QUEEN ANNE.

QUEEN ANNE.

So this is day, a broad, sun-staring day—
And what had it been night? the same, the same.
All time to me is one confusèd mass

Drowned in a flood of bitter misery.
There is no time to one without a hope:
Hopes are the figures on life's changing dial,
That first betray to us the passing hours,
Ere the great bell may summon us away.
All blank and meaningless is life to me:
I have no future. One eternal present,
Rayless as Lapland winter, wraps my soul;
One ceaseless wrong, affording but one sense
Of cruelest agony, makes up my life,
Stretching from day to day its sole event.
What if the sun arise? what if the lark
Put on the glory of his morning song?
What if the flow'rs perk up their loaded heads,
And swing their incense down the thirsting gale?
What if the frame of this whole universe
Warm in the glow, and join the matin hymn?
While I remain in this dull lethargy,
There is no morn to me. Eternal One,
Who sent'st that joyous thing, the rising sun,
As if in mockery of my sullen wo,
To show how cheerless is my nighted soul—
O, end this mere existence! Rouse to life

The fire of my consuming energies!
O, give me scope, and fate-subduing power—
Ay, though a pang be coupled with each act—
Lest, in this trance, the erring scythe of death
Pass o'er my frame, as o'er the trampled grain,
And nature be defeated! Gracious God,
Are we mere puppets of a rigid fate?
Is all this labyrinth of cunning thought
Bestowed to snare us? Must our exit be
Through that one door which destiny holds wide?
To me alone, of all the human race,
Has this dread secret clearly been revealed?
It seems so; for where'er I bend mine eyes
Some ugly phantom bars the hopeless way,
And bids me wait the will of circumstance.
This shall not be! Arise, my drowsing soul!
Gird on thy blazing arms of intellect!
One struggle more to master coming time;
And if thy earthy walls then fall consumed,
We'll scale those heights where conquering time is not!

Enter MARY WYATT.

MARY WYATT.

A fair good morning to your majesty!

QUEEN ANNE.

Welcome, sweet mistress Mary!

MARY WYATT.

Joyful sight!
There is a flush of triumph on your brow,
Such as it wore on coronation day,
Or when the spleenful butcher met his fall.

QUEEN ANNE.

Speak not of Wolsey.

MARY WYATT.

Have I ruffled you?

QUEEN ANNE.

O no, O no! to-day my heart is light.
I feel as if another goodly crown
Hung o'er my head.

MARY WYATT.

Your brother, Rochford, waits.
Since break of day he has been biding here.

QUEEN ANNE.

Ha! what has happened?

MARY WYATT.

Nothing, that I know.

QUEEN ANNE.

Well, well, admit him. [*Exit* MARY WYATT.] Rochford,
at this hour?
A man of ease—and waited here since dawn?
My heart is failing.—Nonsense! what can come,
Worse than the vision of that weak-brained girl
Locked in the circle of my husband's arms?

Enter Viscount ROCHFORD.

Good morrow, Rochford! You are stirring soon.

ROCHFORD.

One stirs betimes who keeps a sleepless night.

QUEEN ANNE.

Have you been ill?

ROCHFORD.

Indeed I cannot tell.
Perchance a fever brought my waking dreams.

QUEEN ANNE.

What dreams?

ROCHFORD.

I lay half slumbering, half awake,
And ever, as my senses leaned to sleep,
The same wild vision roused me from my rest.

QUEEN ANNE.

So you came here, before the break of day,
To tell your dreams? I am no soothsayer.
Pshaw! Rochford, this is trifling. You have griefs,
Big, weighty griefs;—I see them on your brow.

ROCHFORD.

First hear my dream. I swear, no common one,
For you were mingled in it.

QUEEN ANNE.

Well, say on.

ROCHFORD.

I thought, that you and I, for years and years,
Had climbed the rundles of a slippery ladder.
I knew not why we clambered; though above
A blazing halo, like a sunset sky,
Shone glorious, and towards it we bent our steps
Urged by resistless impulse. You were first;

And when I halted, by the labor tired,
Or dizzy at the awful depth beneath,
You cheered me on, and with your nimble feet
Spurned the frail rounds, till sundered 'neath your tread
They fell around me. Woful, woful sight!
Each stick in falling to a ghastly head
Was metamorphosed. Here, Queen Katharine's fell;
There Wolsey's; More's and Fisher's, spouting blood;
And many a one whose face I could not catch.
These, as they passed me, whispered in mine ears
A horrid curse, and grinned, and winked their eyes.—

QUEEN ANNE.

Good heaven, how awful! Was there more of this?

ROCHFORD.

Ay, far more dreadful fancies.

QUEEN ANNE.

Could there be?

ROCHFORD.

Already through the radiant clouds above
Your form was piercing, when our frail support
Shook till I sickened; and aloft I saw

A dreadful shape, in features like the king,
Tugging and straining with his threatening hand
To hurl our ladder to the depths below.
I saw you clutching at the dazzling clouds,
That, unsubstantial, melted in your grasp;
I heard you cry to the unpitying fiend
Who held our lives in his relentless hands;
I saw you turn on me one fearful look,
In whose dread meaning desolate despair
Had crowded all pale shapes of agony,
Ere, with spasmodic catching at my breath,
I shot down headlong.—With the fall, I woke.

QUEEN ANNE.

A fearful dream.

ROCHFORD.

A most connected one.
The thing seems now an uttered prophecy,
Whose power shall bend the neck of stubborn time
To do its bidding.

QUEEN ANNE.

Cheer up, Rochford, cheer!
Some one has told you that his majesty

Looks coldly on me. So has he before,
When I have crossed him in his fiery moods.
To-day, I mean to win him back again.
I must confess I have been negligent,
Not to have closed our matrimonial flaw.

ROCHFORD.

Sister, this levity is forced. I know
That your proud soul has suffered keen chagrin;
Nor in hope's sunshine stand you more than I.
Jane Seymour—

QUEEN ANNE.

Nonsense, man, to place my worth
Against the nothing of so weak a girl.
The king's time lags; his ever-roving eye,
Perchance his appetite, was caught by her:
The eye soon tires, the heart is never full;
The first is hers, the nobler prize is mine.
Hope for the best. If I return to-day
A conquered soldier, from this war of hearts,
I'll give you leave to ease your sorry eyes
O'er my afflictions.

ROCHFORD.

Joy be with you, sister!
Your merry mood has stolen my fear away. (*Going.*)
Yet what I have heard—

QUEEN ANNE.

Nay, what anon you'll hear!

[*Exit* ROCHFORD.

O, misery! to play this queenly part
Even to my brother! To be so supreme
That the sweet flood of human sympathy,
In which the beggar's ragged form may lave,
Can never touch me! This is royalty,
To feel for all that have no sense for me:
To have no kindred, no companionship—
The lonely phœnix on her spicy fire.
Alone, alone! Kind Heaven, the king remains—
My rightful mate, sole partner of my lot—
And I will win him in the throat of death! [*Exit.*

SCENE III.

Another Room in the Palace. Enter KING HENRY *and the Duke of* NORFOLK.

NORFOLK.

Admit the boastings of this silly knave
Are merely grounded on his vanity;
Yet these same boasts, converted to a charge,
Would wear another aspect.

KING HENRY.

Very true;
But 'tis too horrible. Disclose a charge
Less dyed in blackness, bearing yet a colour
Sufficient for divorce, but not for death.
I do believe her a most faithful wife,
Loving and true; though now her tenderness,
Like healthy food to a distempered mouth,
Disgusts the thing 'twould nourish.

NORFOLK.

I am dumb.
I know no charge but what involves a crime
As great as treason. For the lighter fault,
Of secret correspondence with King Francis,
We have no witness, and but scanty grounds
To base our own suspicions on.

KING HENRY.

'Ods wounds!
Would I could rack the French ambassador!
Is there no other way?

NORFOLK.

None, that I know.

KING HENRY.

Then, in the name of all the lying fiends,
Clear out this woman by what means you can!
But mind you, sir, let there be proof enough
To force conviction to the very core
Of mine own conscience.

NORFOLK.

Ah! that tender conscience! (*Aside.*)

Doubt not, my liege; the proof shall be direct.
Suffolk has sent a follower of his,
With three grave witnesses, most truthful men,
To bring Mark Smeaton to that mellow state
In which the tongue o'erleaps the sober will,
And blusters out its secrets.—Truth is a fool,
And drunkenness an artificial folly.

KING HENRY.

Now, by my soul, perchance the charge is true!

NORFOLK.

Doubtless, my liege. Nor is the groom alone
The only evidence may be produced.
I have brought one, a deeply injured wife,
The good Viscountess Rochford; she awaits
Your royal pleasure in the ante-room.

KING HENRY.

"The good Viscountess Rochford!"

NORFOLK.

She can tell
Some wondrous matters to your majesty.

KING HENRY.

Go bring her up. [*Exit* NORFOLK.] "The good Viscountess Rochford!"
If hell were swept, to find its vilest soul,
That soul would blush at sight of this good lady.

Re-enter NORFOLK *with Viscountess* ROCHFORD.

NORFOLK.

I pray your majesty, be gentle with her.
(*Apart to* KING HENRY.)

KING HENRY.

Welcome, my lady!

LADY ROCHFORD.

Heaven protect your highness!

KING HENRY.

His grace of Norfolk says your ladyship
Can tell some wondrous matters of the queen.

LADY ROCHFORD.

Not I, my liege.

KING HENRY.

'Fore heaven! what brought you then?

NORFOLK.

Nay, draw her gently on. She must be led, my liege.
(*Apart to* King Henry.)

KING HENRY.

Who are familiar with her majesty?

LADY ROCHFORD.

Why, Mary Wyatt, and sweet mistress Seymour—

KING HENRY.

Zounds, woman!—and what men?

LADY ROCHFORD.

I know not all.
Besides the Council, and the Churchmen—

KING HENRY.

'Sblood!
And all my army, and my navy too!
Madam, you trifle with us; pray speak out:
I swear no harm shall come, whate'er you say.
What paramours has she? Nay, I command;
Speak, if you love my honor.

LADY ROCHFORD.

Doleful hour,

That I was forced to see her wickedness;
More doleful far, to tell it! Pray, my liege—

KING HENRY.

I'll have no faltering. Speak! or, by high Heaven,
Look to yourself!

LADY ROCHFORD.

I am but a timid woman;
You are my king, and may compel my tongue:
But did not duty—pardon what I say—

KING HENRY.

Enough, enough!

LADY ROCHFORD.

These are her paramours—
Not fancied, but with certainty of proof—
Sir Henry Norris, William Brereton,
Sir Francis Weston, master Thomas Wyatt—
All proper men, all men of gallant parts—

KING HENRY.

We'll spare your comments on the lady's taste.

LADY ROCHFORD.

But there's Mark Smeaton, a low common knave,

By virtue of her favour made a groom;
And last of all, my husband, Viscount Rochford.

KING HENRY.

But he's her brother.

LADY ROCHFORD.

All the worse, my liege.

KING HENRY.

Monstrous! The name that you reserved to crown
The utter horror of this long-drawn list
Throws a discredit on the whole device.
Have you no enemy to name for him?
Have you denounced them all?

LADY ROCHFORD.

I'll prove his guilt
More clearly than the crime of any other.
'Twas but this morn—

KING HENRY.

For God's sake, take her hence!
(*Walks apart.*)

NORFOLK.

The king is satisfied. You may withdraw.
You have pleased him, lady, more than he dare show.
[*Exit Viscountess* ROCHFORD.

KING HENRY.

Must all these die?

NORFOLK.

They all are mortal, sir;
And our fair witness must have that agreed,
Ere she impugns them.

KING HENRY.

Ay, her serpent mouth
Had rather spit its rancorous member forth
Than bate one jot of its malicious spleen:
But Wyatt shall not, Wyatt shall not die.
We have had enough of executing scholars.
Who ever heard such hubbub through the world
As when Sir Thomas More was put to death?
Herod and Pilate were crowned saints to me!
Why, men that looked like moles, old dusty things,
Came from their folios, leaving fear behind,
And to my teeth talked of the infamy

To which they would damn me.—Wyatt shall not die.
In my wide realm are herds of courtiers,
Knights, and viscounts, and gallant gentlemen;
There's but one Wyatt.—Wyatt shall not die! [*Exeunt.*

SCENE IV.

A Room in the Duke of SUFFOLK'S *Palace. Enter Duke of* SUFFOLK, *Duke of* NORFOLK, *Marquis of* EXETER, *and Earl of* ARUNDEL, *followed by* MARK SMEATON *and* RALPH LONEY.

NORFOLK.

I tell you, fellow, you have not a hope,
Save by agreeing to forswear the queen.
Your guilty boastings, urged against your head,
Will bring you to the gallows—

ARUNDEL.

Ay, and shall.

NORFOLK.

Unless before the Council you appear,
And there denounce your royal paramour.

SMEATON.

But will that save me?

NORFOLK.

'Tis your only hope.

SMEATON.

But 'tis a lie—a gross, atrocious lie—
And I am a villain if I uttered it.
Curse on the wine! It was the babbling wine,
And not my tongue, that forged this calumny.

SUFFOLK.

The boast you made was heard by witnesses,
Who say you were but warmed, not drunk with wine.

SMEATON.

'Tis false, 'tis false! Have mercy on me, sirs!
I am but an humble man, of no account;
My death at this time, or a century hence,
Could make no difference to such mighty lords.
If noble mercy stoops not to the low,
At least be just to me.—

ARUNDEL.

Cease whining, cur!

The game we are playing is to check the queen;
What care we for a pawn?

SMEATON.

She is innocent.
The words I dropped were from a foolish whim,
To see myself admired by simple men:
I never thought to injure her, nor hear
My harmless folly rigidly explained
By noblemen. Ah! Loney, you did this;
And 'tis the foulest act you ever did,
Though you have committed murder.

LONEY.

Help yourself.
Be not a double fool, first to get trapped,
Then lack the art to burrow out of harm.
Forget my deeds; they are my own concern;
Nor stand there moralizing on the past.
Seize on to-day—perchance 'tis golden, man.

SMEATON.

"Perchance, perchance!" but not one promise given,
Even by you.

LONEY.

The course they offer you
Is bright with hope; despair and frightful death,
By wrenching tortures and heart-shrivelling fires,
Threaten you darkly from all other ways.
I know your courage. When you have been racked
For one short fortnight, or a month at most,
You'll yield perforce. Why not confess at once,
And gain the hope of pardon and reward?
Pray did you ever see a felon racked,
Even for an hour?

ARUNDEL.

Come, fellow, will you speak?
Or shall I sound your carcass with my sword,
To find your tongue?

EXETER.

The valiant gentleman! (*Aside.*)

SMEATON.

O horror, horror! Have compassion, sirs.
O my poor mistress! Is there not a hand—
Now, while I shut mine eyes—so merciful
As to dispatch me, and deliver her?

She is my maker,—she created me,
From my vile dust, to be whate'er I am:
As well might I blaspheme as stain her honour!
Good sirs, have pity!

SUFFOLK.

Cease your agonies,
You foul-mouthed slanderer of Heaven's majesty!
Speak to the point—will you comply or not?

SMEATON.

But will that save me?

SUFFOLK.

Are we prophets, fool?
What else can save you?

SMEATON.

But her majesty—
What will befall her?

NORFOLK.

What is that to you?
Have you the power to influence her fate?

ARUNDEL.

Are we the answers in your catechism,
That you so glibly question?

SMEATON.

I will not!

SUFFOLK.

Loney, prepare the rack. [*Exit* LONEY.

SMEATON.

Forgive me, Heaven!
I will do anything: but spare my life!
Oh! this is awful! I that never dared
To touch her robe, or raise my fearful eyes
To the full glory of her angel face—
When her twin orbs of conquering majesty
I felt upon me—now, with stubborn front,
To stand before the gaze of frowning Heaven,
And call its host to register a lie,—
A black, soul-killing lie! O, urge it not!
There 's not an honest man in England's realm
Who will not sicken at my perfidy,
Or cram the falsehood down my caitiff throat

Ere I half utter it! This is too foul,
And useless for the end to which you urge it.

SUFFOLK.

Loney, the rack.

(A curtain is drawn, and the rack disclosed, with Attendants standing near it.)

ARUNDEL.

Look there, Sir Constancy!
There's what shall move you, every joint and limb—
There's what shall stretch you more than you'll stretch truth.
You'll strain a point for this—hey! hey! my boy?

SMEATON.

O, nerve me, Heaven!—uplift my faltering heart!
Give me the strength to foil these sinful men,
And here assert thy might!

ARUNDEL.

Away with him!

(Attendants seize SMEATON.*)*

SMEATON.

I yield, I yield!

SUFFOLK.

Then sign this paper, Mark;
And wait the issue. (SMEATON *signs.*)

EXETER.

There an angel fell!
Here is a wretch who damns his endless soul
To save his mortal body. I had hoped,
For the poor cause of frail humanity,
To see yon fellow win a martyr's crown,
And give the Calendar of our new creed
Its first accomplished sainthood. (*Aside.*)

SUFFOLK.

It is done.

NORFOLK.

In the king's name, Mark Smeaton I arrest
For treason manifest. (*Attendants seize* SMEATON.)

SMEATON.

Is this your mercy?

SUFFOLK.

Traitor, no words! Away with him, away! [*Exeunt.*

SCENE V.

An Apartment in Whitehall Palace. Enter KING HENRY.

KING HENRY.

How easy 'tis to run an evil course,
How many stubborn checks a virtuous meets!
Sure all the fiends have turned them engineers,
And smoothed the thousand pathways to their gulf,
So quickly trod by man. There's not a let,
As far as reason's straining eye can pierce,
To the career which sin points out for me.
Jane daily warms; the queen grows proud and cold,
Nor now besieges me with tender notes;
My nobles leave her, all afire for me;
And the most powerful—ay, her very kin—
Hatch plots to work her sudden overthrow.
My love goes smoothly.—Hum! and yet 'tis strange,
When not within the circle of mine eyes—
That drink her beauties like the thirsting sands,
And bear the hot thrill of her loveliness

Into my very soul—how this same fever,
That fiercely glowed erewhile, calms and is cooled;
How in the place of sudden pangs and starts,
And all unrest, a holy peace succeeds;
When comes the shape of my much wrongéd queen,
Crossing my mind in quiet majesty,
And trampling on the dust of noxious fancies,
That throng the long, long avenues of thought,
As if of right she crushed my base desires.

Enter QUEEN ANNE, *behind.*

QUEEN ANNE.

Henry.

KING HENRY.

Was that a spirit?

QUEEN ANNE.

Husband, king.

KING HENRY.

How came you here? I had left strict command
That no one should disturb my privacy.
Have you again been tampering with my knaves?

QUEEN ANNE.

I came by a small passage—if forgot
By you, my liege, still to my memory dear—
Made by yourself, in that once happy time,
When, unobserved, you came to woo "The Boleyn."
Is there no secret passage, you can tell,
Through which so poor a one as I may creep
Back to your heart, and see again the face
Of hidden love? O, sir, it must be rough,
And small, and frightful to a valiant gaze,
But I will tempt it.

KING HENRY.

There is none for you.
Your pride, and haughtiness, and stubborn will
Are all too big for love's slight passages.—
Now, by my faith, I am indeed amazed,
To hear you pleading in this gentle tone.
Have you forgot your character? Begin!
Rail, like the thunders, at our guilty world!
So ho! brave censor of morality,
Embodied purity, untouched by earth—
What, are you pitiful? or have you sinned,
And therefore feel compassion?

QUEEN ANNE.

I have sinned,
And tried the mercy of indulgent Heaven
Beyond all bounds that human reason knows.
I have been arrogant, to judge my kind
By God's own law, not seeing in myself
A guilty judge condemning the less vile.
I have forgotten that the hand of death
Would snatch the royal circle from my brow,
And set me, but encumbered by my guilt,
Equal with all, before the judgment seat.
I have forgotten mercy: so might God
Forget His mercy in my utmost need.
I have—

KING HENRY.

Hoot! madam; pray restrain yourself!
I have no office to receive confessions.
Yet—since you force me to play ghostly father—
Is there no other sin, of grosser cast,
By you committed, not towards Heaven alone,
But to my honour?

QUEEN ANNE.

'Tis a hideous lie!
Who has abused your majesty's belief
With such unworthy tattle? Did you stand
And tamely hear your honour thus belied?
I knew that I had enemies enough,
Unscrupulous and cruel; but never deemed
Such base, malicious, and unfounded charge
Could move a human lip, or find an ear,
So used to gorging sickly mental stuff,
As to receive it. Try me, try me, sir.
Wring every fibre of my woman's frame
With piercing tortures—hold my modesty,
In truth's keen sunlight, to the vulgar gaze—
Confront me crownless with my slanderers:
If at the last my trial prove me clear,
And reunite our long-dissevered hearts,
I'll hold the pain but lightly.

KING HENRY.

Pshaw! my child,
You waste your energy. This base report
Is the light mintage of some idle tongue,
In want of truer metal.

QUEEN ANNE.

Ah! my liege,
I hold this shallow falsehood at its worth;
But it afflicts me sadly, to behold
Your easy method of avoiding it,
Without a thought of punishing the wrong.
How have I changed?—O, Henry, you have changed
From that true Henry who, in bygone days,
Rode, with the hurry of a northern gale,
Towards Hever's heights, and ere the park was gained,
Made the glad air a messenger of love,
By many a blast upon your hunting-horn.
Have you forgotten that old oaken room,
Fearful with portraits of my buried race,
Where I received you panting from your horse;
As breathless, from my dumb excess of joy,
As you with hasty travel? Do you think
Of our sweet meetings 'neath the gloomy yews
Of Sopewell nunnery, when the happy day
That made me yours seemed lingering as it came,
More slowly moving as it nearer drew?
How you chid time, and vowed the hoary knave
Might mark each second of his horologe

With dying groans, from those you cherished most,
So he would hasten?—

KING HENRY.

Anne, that was you.
Have you forgotten my ear-stunning laugh
At your quaint figure of time's human clock,
Whose every beat a soul's flight registered?

QUEEN ANNE.

God bless you, Henry! (*Embraces him.*)

KING HENRY.

Pshaw! why touch so deep?
These softening memories of our early love
Come o'er me like my childhood.

QUEEN ANNE.

Love be praised,
That with such pure reflections couples me!
Be steadfast, Henry.

KING HENRY.

Fear not: love is poor
That seals not compacts with the stamp of faith.

QUEEN ANNE.

My stay is trespass. We will meet anon.
Love needs no counsel in his little realm.

[*Embraces him, and exit.*

KING HENRY.

I hang 'tween heaven and hell.—Anne, return;
For, by my soul, one half my virtuous strength
Has gone with you! O I had rather be
The snarling cynic in his squalid tub,
And master of myself, than England's king,
Reared to indulgence of each flimsy whim
That passion hints at. 'Tis the curse of kings,
This slaving to our pampered appetites;
Which thwarted men nursed in vicissitude,
And by compulsion taught to check desire,
Gain strength to vanquish.

Enter JANE SEYMOUR.

JANE SEYMOUR.

Harry, royal Harry!

KING HENRY.

Good morrow, mistress Seymour.

JANE SEYMOUR.

Ha! so cold—
The queen just gone! I'll match you, whirligig. (*Aside.*)
I crave your pardon, that with rude alarm
I thus disturbed your gracious majesty,
Seeking for one I nicknamed royal Harry—
Not meaning disrespect to you, my liege,
But from a wanton fancy. Had I thought
Your majesty here present, I had held
A stricter rein upon my noisy tongue.

KING HENRY.

Ah! she is beautiful. This little mood,
Of mingled coquetry and tearful spite,
Sits like the angry rain-drops on a rose,
Giving fresh lustre to its crimson cheeks. (*Aside.*)
You have my pardon.

JANE SEYMOUR.

Nay, I wish it not.
Pray cast your pardon on a graver slip:
Forgive the maiden greenness of a heart
That prattled to itself a silly tale

Of love, and hope, and thoughtless confidence,
Even in your very presence.

KING HENRY.

Jane, what mean you?

JANE SEYMOUR.

But what my words imply.

KING HENRY.

And are you angry?

JANE SEYMOUR.

No, I am deceived.

KING HENRY.

Truce, truce, fair mistress!

JANE SEYMOUR.

Nay, peace is not my purpose.

KING HENRY.

Prithee stop!

JANE SEYMOUR.

You may be king of half the universe,

For aught I care; you are not king of hearts:
My heart shall speak, though every word cry treason!

KING HENRY.

Forgive my coldness.

JANE SEYMOUR.

O, I never deemed
A truer spirit lived than yours, my liege:
Else why did you, from your exalted height,
Descend with flattering promises of love?—
Only to make me wretched! O 'tis base!
A brutal hind might show more constancy
Than this anointed king. (*Weeps.*)

KING HENRY.

Nay, weep not, Jane. (*Kneels.*)
See me thus lowly in my penitence.
I swear I meant no insult to you, darling;
And here, upon my knees, I once again
Put on the easy fetters of my heart.

JANE SEYMOUR.

Swear fealty to love: Your fickleness

Reproaches more your manly character
Than the poor wrong to me—

KING HENRY.

I swear, by Heaven,
Henceforth to love you with all constancy,
By night, by day, in sunshine and in storm;
Nor will I alter in my steadfast aim
To crown you queen, though every mortal sin,
That fiends can reckon in their calendar,
Lies between me and my unfaltering wish! (*Rises.*)

JANE SEYMOUR.

This oath is fearful.

KING HENRY.

But irrevocable.—
What ask you more?

JANE SEYMOUR.

O, sir, I asked not that:
I but demand of you a bare return
For the great venture of my woman's heart,
Unhappily launched upon a sea of love,

With you for careless pilot. 'Tis my all;
Though you esteem the charge of little worth.

KING HENRY.

Tut, tut! my darling; if our hearts respond,
Our windy tongues are poor ambassadors
To bear their gentle greetings. Love is dumb,
A potent spirit, felt, but never heard,
Save when he murmurs inarticulate
'Tween meeting lips, or buzzes wild conceits,
That mock the language of our grosser sense,
In lovers' brains. Words are love's counterfeits:
When stumbling fools would ape a shallow passion,
Lies slide full glibly, and false rhetoric,
Lashed to a foam, roars opposition down,
And for effect kills feeling. Rail no more;
Or I shall doubt that sweet sincerity
On which I live.

JANE SEYMOUR.

O, never doubt my faith.

KING HENRY.

Nor will I. (*Embraces her.*) I will bar my pliant ears
Against the witchery of sly Anne's tongue:

Her airy magic cheats my spell-bound heart,
And for a moment shows a fancied spot,
Bright with the May-day flowers of early love,
Amid December's snow. And now for Norfolk.

JANE SEYMOUR.

Nothing in haste, my liege.

KING HENRY.

No; all in love.

[*Exeunt.*

ACT IV.

SCENE I. *The Lists at Greenwich, prepared for a Tournament. Flourish. Enter* KING HENRY, QUEEN ANNE, *Lords, Ladies, Attendants, Men-at-arms, &c. The King and Queen seat themselves under the cloth of state. Then enter the lists Viscount* ROCHFORD *and other Knights, as Challengers, with Heralds, Squires, Pages, &c. Trumpets sound a challenge. To them enter Sir* HENRY NORRIS *and other Knights, as Defenders, with Attendants, &c. Flourish.* ROCHFORD, NORRIS, *and their respective Knights engage.* NORRIS *and his party are driven back.*

QUEEN ANNE.

I pray your highness, let them breathe awhile;
Their sport grows earnest. Ill may come of this:
Rochford is dangerous when his blood is up.

KING HENRY.

Poh! poh! mere bruises. Would you rather see
Rochford or Norris murdered?

QUEEN ANNE.

Neither, neither!—
Good sir, 'tis frightful.

KING HENRY.

Ha! so kind to both?
Then love admits not of relationship.

QUEEN ANNE.

Sound, herald, sound!

(*Trumpets sound a retreat, and the combat ceases.*)

KING HENRY.

Now, by the holy rood! (*Starts up.*)
If we were speechless, Heaven had been most kind
In sending one to exercise our function.

QUEEN ANNE.

I feared, my liege—

KING HENRY.

O, this is nothing new:
You have governed England, me amongst the rest,
Since God knows when!—You thing of painted cloth,
When next you blow without your king's command,

Look to your tabard.—Is our queen our tongue?

(QUEEN ANNE, *in her terror, drops her handkerchief.* NORRIS *picks it up, kisses, and returns it.*)

Monstrous, by Jove! What, in our very presence!—
Shameless adulteress! Let the tilt be stopped!
We are as patient as most ill-used men,
But this we cannot bear. Set on, before!
Was ever king thus openly defied? [*Exit with Courtiers.*

QUEEN ANNE.

Oh! horror, horror! (*She faints, and is borne off.*)

ROCHFORD.

Norris, did I hear?
Or am I singled from among you all
To bear the terrors of this fantasy?

NORRIS.

Alas! your senses serve too faithfully:
Would I could doubt you sane!

Enter THOMAS WYATT, *hastily.*

WYATT.

Fly, Rochford, fly!
And you, Sir Henry Norris, if you'd live.

NORRIS.

I fly! and wherefore?

WYATT.

Ask not, but away—
Away to Scotland; nor till every inch
Of English ground has vanished from your sight,
Draw rein or spare the spur!

ROCHFORD.

Oh! I am stunned
With dull intensity of present grief;
No after blow, that cuts my torpid soul
Loose from its clay, can bear a pang for me!
I will not fly to live. I have beheld
A sight to force me into love with death—
The most unkingly, meanest, foulest deed
That brother's eyes e'er saw.

WYATT.

Now 'tis too late.

Enter an OFFICER *and* GUARD.

OFFICER.

Lord Rochford and Sir Henry Norris, yield!

I do arrest you for high treason, sirs.
Give up your arms, and follow to the Tower.

ROCHFORD.

Yes, yes. Come, Norris; for I make no doubt,
What was our virtue has become our guilt:
Love to the queen is treason to the king.
When the great fall the little must be crushed.

NORRIS.

Wyatt, what means this? I accused of treason!

WYATT.

Ay, 'tis a royal charge!

NORRIS.

Ha! say you so?
Had you this order from his majesty,
Or from the Council? (*To the* OFFICER.)

OFFICER.

From the king direct.
Come, gentlemen; my office stands in peril
By my indulgence to you.

ROCHFORD.

Farewell! Wyatt.

NORRIS.

My lord, be not down-hearted. This affair
Will soon blow over.

ROCHFORD.

Yes, to other men;
But I much fear that on my latest day
It will have reached its climax.

OFFICER.

Come, sirs, come!

WYATT.

Heaven send your innocence a quick release!

ROCHFORD.

With death to bear the warrant.

[*Exeunt* ROCHFORD, NORRIS, OFFICER, *and* GUARD.

WYATT.

So I fear,
Doomed victims of a ruthless tyranny.
O, coming shape of English liberty,

Have my desires played wanton to mine ears?
Or do I hear the faint prophetic sound
Of thine approaching footsteps echoing through
The mists of coming time? Ye noble souls,
Grim heroes of the field of Runnymede,
Showing more glorious in your iron arms,
On peaceful deeds, than in successful wars—
Inspire the souls of your too slothful race!
Must all the liberty your courage won
Slip from the hands to which you rendered it;
Till the supineness of our base neglect
Sink us to slaves? Is there no man alive—
No heaven-marked hero, from the people sprung—
To lead the roaring multitudes of earth
Along the fated pathway they must tread—
Ay, though they cross the throne, and trample out
The sacred name and dignity of king?
Has man no rights but what a tyrant doles?—
No fate above his will? no claim on justice?
Then doth God wrong His own dread sovereignty;
For He has sworn to render mankind right,
Even against Himself. And she has fallen,
Sole star amid this night of tyranny—

How low I know not; but the shallowest depth
A queen may fall is deeper than the grave.
I feel my weakness to support her cause,
Even though my mounting soul could touch the sun,
Against this pampered monster of a king—
This frightful idol of the people's will,
Throned on the superstitious reverence
Of the poor fools that glut his savage maw.
O what a curse to have an honest heart,
Hemmed in and cramped by the fixed frame of things,
That, were it free, might move the stubborn world,
And hang its glories on the brow of time! [*Exit.*

SCENE II.

A Room in the Palace of Whitehall. Enter KING HENRY.

KING HENRY.

Too late, too late! I charged her openly;
The issue now lies between her and me,
And not between her innocence and guilt.
I am a villain, or the queen is false,

Since I became accuser of her truth:
If she escape conviction, on the crown
Descends the infamy of calumny,
And through our person England will be shamed
Before the jealous powers of Christendom.
So, so! we owe it to our people then
To prove our charge, or by conviction sure
Seem to attest it.—This is plain enough.
Besides, in what regard stands common life
Before our kingly honour? Julius said
That Cæsar's wife must be without a taint;
And, but suspecting, put Pompeia by.—
Wise Cæsar! 'twas a solemn precedent
That kings should follow. Wherefore halt I now?
A limping purpose never reached its mark,
Though justice pointed. Should her guilt be proved?—
Should an impartial court of noble peers
Condemn her too? O woful, woful thought!
How shall I pardon her gross treachery?
Their candid verdict will stop pity's ears,
And force conviction to my doubting mind.
She shall have trial, fair and open trial—
No honest men would wrong the innocent;

And if they do?—her blood but swells their crimes;
I escape stainless.

Enter Sir Henry Norris *in custody of* Officer *and* Guard.

Officer, withdraw;
But stand in hail. [*Exeunt* Officer *and* Guard.] Ah!
Norris, Henry Norris,
You have abused that open confidence
In which we held you.

NORRIS.

I! and how, my liege?

KING HENRY.

Nay, strive not, sir, to hide your secret guilt
With artful candour and affected starts.
Sin can put on the guise of innocence;
Nor ever cheats us with its ugliness,
But with its seeming beauty.

NORRIS.

On my life,
I know not to what sin your tongue directs.

KING HENRY.

Have you not wronged me?

NORRIS.

Wrongged your majesty!

KING HENRY.

Yes; have you not, to swell your amorous triumphs,
And make yourself an envied libertine,
Seduced the virtue of our fickle queen?

NORRIS.

Your grace is merry. (*Laughing.*)

KING HENRY.

"Merry!" are you mad?
I say it can be proved.

NORRIS.

"Proved!" Set the hound,
That howled this lying folly in your ears,
Within the reach of my chastising sword,
And if I send him not to fiery hell,
With his foul tattle warm upon his lips,
Rack me to powder!

KING HENRY.

Acted to the life!

NORRIS.

O no, my liege; 'tis but the natural heat
That would boil over every English lip,
To hear their queen traduced.

KING HENRY.

Be calm, Sir Harry.
So much we hold the honour of our realm
Before the vengeance due to private wrongs,
That we have vowed to bury our own grief,
And grant free pardon to whatever man—
Even though he were her fondest paramour—
Will fix the crime upon her guilty head.

NORRIS.

I am not he. I thought, until this hour—
Ay, and still think, and will, despite report—
Our queen as loyal to your majesty
As the chaste moon is to her regal sun,
Drinking no other beams. What though she shine
Upon the darkness of our grateful earth,
To cheer the spirits of night-foundered men?—
That which she gives, she borrows from yourself;

Fruitful to her, but, when it falls on us,
The calm, cold splendour of reflected light.

KING HENRY.

Norris, beware! you carry this too far:
If you confess not, instant, shameful death
Awaits your stubborn spirit.

NORRIS.

Be it so:
I'll rather add a thousand stings to death,
Than give one pang to suffering innocence.

KING HENRY.

Then be it so, you contumacious boy!
Have I embraced you in my trusting heart,
To be denied when I demand return?

NORRIS.

Ha! do I hear? What saw your majesty,
Even in so poor a man as Henry Norris,
To make you hold me for a supple tool
To work your bloody purpose? You must go
A step below a knight and gentleman,
To find a villain fitted to your wish.

KING HENRY.

Poh! poh! coy virtue, is it villainous
To show obedience when your king commands?

NORRIS.

Is there no power in every honest breast,
Above the terrors of your threatening will,
'Neath whose fixed look my guilty memory
Shall cower in horror?

KING HENRY.

You must do this deed.—
Nay, I adjure you.

NORRIS.

O, my gracious liege—

KING HENRY.

No words, no words!

NORRIS.

Avaunt, damned hypocrite!
I here defy your utmost reach of wrath:
The cruelest death your wickedness can shape
Would be a joy to what you offer me.
Stretch your base tortures through all coming time,

And in the end they can but kill my clay;
But you would turn my hand to impious use,
And make me, like a frantic suicide,
Stab at the roots of mine eternal soul—
That, by God's blessing, shall outlast your hate,
And reign triumphant when your crown is dross!

KING HENRY.

Hold, villain, hold! or I will let the breath
Out of your treacherous body! (*Draws.*)

NORRIS.

Do, my liege,
And join assassination to the crimes
That blot your monstrous heart.—I will not hold:
I see you are bent upon destroying me,
And as a reckless man I'll know your worst.
O wo to England, when this sinful king,
Grown hard in crime, shall reach the fearful height
That evil points him! Then shall—

KING HENRY.

Brazen traitor!
Dare you invoke our vengeance on your head?

Without there! (*Re-enter* OFFICER *and* GUARD.) See
your prisoner to the Tower.
If he escape, you had better hang yourselves
Than live to tell it. Out, malignant traitor!

[*Exit Sir* HENRY NORRIS, *in custody of the* GUARD.

O the ingratitude of fickle man!
The shifting sand that tumbles in the tide,
Taking new form from every wanton surge,
Is not more changeful than his rootless heart.
He is a bark upon an angry sea,
Unballasted, yet ever crowding sail;
Careening now to passion's fiery gust,
Now to the other side prostrated flat
By self-styled reason's icy hurricane;
Yet never sailing on an even keel—
Ever extreme, and no extreme the best.
Who that had seen the favours I have showered,
As thick and prodigal as Spring's warm sun,
Upon the head of that remorseless wretch,
Could have foreknown the desert barrenness
Of his rude heart!—Pah! I am sick of it.
O the ingratitude of wicked man! [*Exit.*

SCENE III.

The Queen's Apartments in the Palace. QUEEN ANNE *and* MARY WYATT.

QUEEN ANNE.

No audience, said you?

MARY WYATT.

None, your highness, nonc.

QUEEN ANNE.

But are you sure his majesty refused
To read my letter?

MARY WYATT.

Very sure; or whence
The new-sprung insolence of every groom?
They passed me by, for nigh a weary hour,
Without observance. When at length I spoke,
Demanding audience in your highness' name,
They almost thrust me from the ante-room,
With taunts and sneers. One knave, a malpert page,

By you presented to his majesty,
Said, with his arms akimbo, in a style
That mimicked the king's bearing—"Mistress Mary,
When we desire to know of blubbering spells,
At your sad corner of our merry house,
We'll come to seek them;—till that time, adieu!"
At this his fellows grinned, like tickled apes,
And winked, and leered at me; till I abashed,
More that such things were human, than for fear
Of any shame their insults might provoke,
Came sadly here, my mission unachieved.

QUEEN ANNE.

I blame you not: I trusted in your zeal,
Knowing its failure set all hope aside
Save that which harbours in myself. Must I
Again go begging for his chary love,
After the public shame he put me to?
Must I go whimpering like a stricken cur—
I who am wronged, and should demand redress—
And pray, in mercy to my feebleness,
This blow may be the last? Degrading thought!
Were I the housewife of his lowest clown,

Caned to obedience by a drunkard's hand,
My woman's heart has in it pride enough
To burst ere bear this last humility.

MARY WYATT.

If pity move him—

QUEEN ANNE.

"Pity!" there is a shame,
More fearful in its furious rebuke,
That follows threatening on the heels of wrong—
An earthly hell in which the conscience writhes,
And lashes round its fiery barrier,
Till suffering purifies the tortured soul;—
This he must feel, ere meek-eyed pity's hand
Will ope the silver gates of penitence,
And through forgiveness show the way to peace.

MARY WYATT.

O may he feel it!

QUEEN ANNE.

"Feel it!" he is human.

MARY WYATT.

Yes; but before some heavier injury
Makes pity useless.

QUEEN ANNE.

Pray, speak plainly, girl!
I see your heart is big with mystery.
What new misfortune is about to fall?

MARY WYATT.

None, as I hope.

QUEEN ANNE.

Nay, this is churlishness:
You have some secret that may profit me.
If I am ignorant of coming ills,
How shall I guard me with expedients
Against their wrath? The man by death assailed
Is last to know the danger he is in.
I make no doubt, but half the palace lackeys
Have drawn a surer presage of my fate,
From buzzing rumour, could more truly mark
What will befal me for a year to come,
Than I, with my own lot to outward seeming

Within my grasp, could compass by design.
So hangs our fate upon the breath of all,
That oft a rumour shapes the destiny
Of feeble wills.

MARY WYATT.

'Twould but fatigue your ears,
Not profit you, to hear the thousand woes
That fools predict upon your majesty:
But there's much comfort in the croak of folly.

QUEEN ANNE.

O, merely thus? naught in particular?
Well, let them rail; the gale is adverse now,
I must expect this dash of saucy spray
Full in my face: anon the wind will change;
Then they'll come tripping to my very heels,
Sparkling with joy, and glad to decorate
My rearward path.

MARY WYATT.

Heaven guard your cheerful mind!

QUEEN ANNE.

Actions begun in cheerfulness, display

The merry herald that foreruns success.
The smile that lights an earnest countenance
Seems as a gleam from some vast mental fire
That burns within, and ever flashes out,
Like tropic lightning on a summer night;
Harmless indeed, yet hinting of a power
That, moved to wrath, might shake the seated earth.
To sulk at sorrow dulls the edge of will,
And half unfits us for prosperity;
Much more for danger, where each faculty
That gives us sway is needed at its full.

MARY WYATT.

When took your highness to philosophy?

QUEEN ANNE.

Ha! you malicious elf! When heavy griefs
First leaguered my poor heart, through it I found
A path to wander from perplexing fears,
That lost in speculation dismal self.
Sorrow makes many a deep philosopher.
Far-reaching thought and his blithe offspring hope
Are leech and nurse to morbid memory.

MARY WYATT.

Great minds may carry a great load unbowed.
Ah me! it brings me to my woman's part,
To hear these strains of sweet philosophy
Rise from her injured spirit. (*Aside, weeping.*) Sure the God
Who suffers mischief to afflict you thus,
Gives you the strength to bear it.

QUEEN ANNE.

Doubtless, doubtless.

Enter THOMAS WYATT.

MARY WYATT.

My brother, please you. [*Retires.*

QUEEN ANNE.

Ah! good master Wyatt—
What news abroad? Why do you shake your head?—
Why wear that funeral face? It seems to me
That all my friends would plunder me of grief.
Came you alone? Where are my other friends?

WYATT.

Gone with the summer flies. The day is dark;
And they that erewhile revelled in your light,
Now sluggish hide in close obscurity,
And prophesy of falling weather soon.

QUEEN ANNE.

But Rochford? he is true in sun or shade.

WYATT.

Ay, by my soul! And know you not?

QUEEN ANNE.

Not I.

WYATT.

Indeed?—That I should bear the intelligence!

QUEEN ANNE.

These dread inductions to ill-omened news
Pitch swift imagination far below
The heaviest fact. Out with it, tender sir!—
What ever saw you like a fear in me?

WYATT.

Lodged in the Tower.

QUEEN ANNE.

A prisoner! on what charge?

WYATT.

A charge as common now as larceny,—
High treason.

QUEEN ANNE.

Treason! who is loyal then?
O what a shallow matter for arrest!
Poor Rochford!—This is strange.—How bears he it?

WYATT.

As innocence e'er bears calamity,—
Suffering in body, but content at heart.

QUEEN ANNE.

I'll to the king. Are not my wrongs enough,
But that my foes must vex my kindred too?
For Rochford's sake, I'll quell my stubborn pride,
And ask the justice I deny myself.

WYATT.

O would you might! See you yon sentinel
Who counts his steps along the corridor?

That knave has orders from his majesty,
On no account to let your highness pass.

QUEEN ANNE.

Good sir, what augurs this? I feel it here—
Here at my heart—a quaking like the step
Of some advancing doom. 'Tis terrible,
To be environed by an enemy
Whose very aims are hidden. Give me light!
O, Wyatt, show me but my coward foes,
Though they are numberless as Egypt's plague—
Let me but see the weapons in their hands,
Though they can blast the angry Thunderer,
And I'll confront them! But to be assailed
By arrows that seem raining from the clouds—
To see my tribe, like Niobe's, cut down,
Nor know what time my breast may be transfixed—
To feel myself the cause of all this wo,
Without the chance of offering stroke for stroke,
Is next to madness!

WYATT.

All I know is this,—
Lord Rochford, Norris, Brereton and Weston,

As the most noted followers of your highness,
Have been arrested, charged with secret treason.
In what particulars their guilt consists,
Even wakeful rumour has not been informed;
Nor are the prisoners wiser than the world.
That popinjay, Mark Smeaton, too, has had
Some private hearings in the council-room,
After a tampering which he underwent
At Suffolk's house.

QUEEN ANNE.

No more of him;—he is harmless.
All these brave hearts to suffer for my sake!
O deadly cowards! to remove these props,
Whose sturdy valour might have long upheld
Even the structure of a tottering cause.

WYATT.

Whatever scheme your enemies have formed
Is now converted to a state affair:
Your highness therefore must expect a blow,
Not from the lords Suffolk, Norfolk, and their friends,
But from the Council.

QUEEN ANNE.

Let them only come!
My heart is aching to begin the fray:
I vow, the conquered shall not fight again!
What of the king?

WYATT.

His majesty is silent,
Gloomy and sad, and given to muttering;
Flying at pleasures with an eagerness
That crushes out the dainty soul of joy:
As one a cup of rich, untasted wine
Might crack with furious bacchanalian haste,
And spill its fruity treasures.

QUEEN ANNE.

So I thought:
His love is wrestling with an agony,
By fancied justice thrust upon his mind.
When through this fire of malice I have passed—
Whose purifying ordeal he allows,
Only to prove the temper of my heart—
Look, Wyatt, look to see mine enemies,
Drossy with crime, hurled headlong in the flame,

To show the baseness of their earthy souls!
Kings should be just.

WYATT.

Ay, should be just.

QUEEN ANNE.

How now?
Would you arraign his royal qualities,
Because my foes have led his mind astray
With seeming justice? O be careful, sir,
Not to malign him, in your zeal for me!

WYATT.

She hugs her ruin. (*Aside.*) Mistress Seymour says—

QUEEN ANNE.

Out, wizard, out! Dare you to summon up
The horrid phantom that pursues my steps,
And ever shadowy flits before mine eyes,
Veiling the sun, and deepening deepest night?
O Wyatt, Wyatt, would you mock me too?
O would you rend the feeble barrier
That hides mine anguish from the gaping world,
And show me in my naked wretchedness,

Without a rag of pride to cover me,
For prying fools to carp on? Cruel leech,
To probe this wound, even though my tortured heart
Might work salvation out of agony.
Begone, begone!

WYATT.

I meant not—

QUEEN ANNE.

I forgive you.
Go, go, in mercy! If you love my health,
Never again recall that fearful name. [*Exit* WYATT.
'Tis hard, 'tis hard!—but it must be endured.
O vanished peace, that with my girlish hours
Shook hands and parted, as they proudly strode
Down the dark paths of untried womanhood,—
Return, return! O couldst thou bring again
Those pleasant days, when at the source of life
My spirit sat, and heard, with nature's tones,
The blended music of a higher life
Mix and flow on in one grand harmony;
When every sense, content with what it felt,
Longed not for action, never-ending action,

That once embraced makes us its slaves till death.—
Death, death! There is more sweetness in that name
Than I e'er knew of. Does thy pallid hand
Unite the two extremes of human life,
Linking our earliest with our latest days,
In one unbroken circle? Art thou she,
The meek-faced peace of childhood, changed in name,
But undistinguished in thy quality,
Come from afar to lead us back again
From where we started? Ah! I know not now,
Nor can I till I pass, beyond recall,
The narrow lintel of the voiceless grave.—
Oh God! oh God! I am weary of the day!

[*Scene closes.*

SCENE IV.

Another Room in the Palace. Enter King Henry *and* Jane Seymour.

KING HENRY.

Poh! 'tis too late for pity.

JANE SEYMOUR.

"Pity," sir!
I feel no pity for her wantonness:
'Tis for yourself, so wickedly abused,
So unsuspecting till the common voice
Thrust its belief in your reluctant ears.
The hand of justice is in everything:
How strange it was our budding love put forth
Just as her impious crimes had reached their full!
Showing how Heaven may visit secret guilt
In an avenging form of innocence,
That sadly marvels at its own result.

KING HENRY.

Yes, very strange.

JANE SEYMOUR.

What proof can be produced?
A mind so subtle in committing sin,
Must be adept in masking stratagems.

KING HENRY.

That's Norfolk's part. His grace has pledged himself
To bring more evidence before the court—

Uncircumstantial, downright, stubborn proof—
Than it will hear. And let him look to it:
For if his charge prove slander to our queen,
And she escape, untainted in her fame,
I'll hang him like a thief—by Heaven, I will!

JANE SEYMOUR.

Sweet hypocrite! (*Aside.*) But if his charge be proved?

KING HENRY.

Our realm has laws; too much we honour them,
To stand between the culprit and their doom.
Talk not of this.

JANE SEYMOUR.

Here comes the noble duke,
Sending a smile before his onward path
To ask a welcome.

Enter Duke of NORFOLK.

NORFOLK.

All looks fair, my liege.

KING HENRY.

Looks foul, I say! Cannot I teach you, sir,

That this discovered treachery of the queen
Irks me to credit? Is it not enough,
That the dear honour of my father's throne
Is sullied in the eyes of Christendom,
And I am made the laughing-stock of time,
Without this giggling at my sorry plight?

NORFOLK.

A virtuous mood! (*Aside.*) Pardon the clownish haste
That has disturbed your majesty's deep grief.
You set me to pursue a wily chase;
And if I feel the huntsman's eager flush—
More from pursuit than wish to strike my game—
The heat of triumph should excuse my air.

KING HENRY.

Well, well,—what news?

NORFOLK.

So ho! king weathercock!
(*Aside.*)

I fear 'tis too much for your majesty
To hear the worst confirmed.

KING HENRY.

Ha! say you so?
For to drift on upon a level sea
Of settled wo, is better than to toss
Between the heights of my delusive hopes
And the deep gulfs of bottomless despair.
Rest, Norfolk, rest from my o'erwhelming thoughts,
Even in a port of quiet wretchedness,
Would be a pleasure to this spirit-storm.

NORFOLK.

There is not a circumstance or shade of proof,
By law demanded to convict the queen,
But I can summon to outface her tongue.
This is blunt truth, ungarbled by a phrase
To smooth its meaning in a dainty ear;
And though you shrink, your royal dignity
Calls out for vengeance on her traitorous head.

KING HENRY.

Be well prepared: your life hangs by a thread.

NORFOLK.

I see your snares, sceptred duplicity;

I am fairly entered, far beyond retreat:
I know the issue is her death or mine.
Thank Heaven, I do not need fear's ragged spur
To drive me onward in my willing course. (*Aside.*)
Trust to my zeal; I hold my sovereign's honour
Above the selfish dread of common death.

KING HENRY.

What of this spinnet player?

NORFOLK.

Ah! the knave!
He wavered sadly since his first confession:
Now he'd confirm the paper which he signed,
And now he'd suffer death ere swear to it.
When strict imprisonment had cowed his mind,
I by persuasion won him to my wish.

KING HENRY.

By what persuasion? Make no promises;
The wretch shall hang.

NORFOLK.

O, merely by the rack.

KING HENRY.

Most delicate inducement!

NORFOLK.

Yes, my liege,
It oft unclasps the rigid jaws of guilt.
The pangs of death have many a time disclosed
The murderer's secret; and the rack can bring
A dying anguish, without fear of death.
'Tis a most potent questioner.

JANE SEYMOUR.

My liege,
Pray come away; for I am sick at heart,
Hearing details so awful. Please, your grace,
To keep such horrors for your private thoughts.
Come, Henry, come!

KING HENRY.

To please you, love. Adieu!
Good Norfolk; slack not in your zealous care.

NORFOLK.

Heaven keep your majesties!

JANE SEYMOUR.

Pshaw! trifler.

[*Exeunt* KING HENRY *and* JANE SEYMOUR.

NORFOLK.

"Pshaw!"

But did I tickle you, my demi-queen?
So delicate, so royal in your tastes!
Cannot endure the thoughts of brutal racks;
And yet would kill a queen to wear her shoes!
'Sdeath! when you are crowned, our manly swords must rust,
Butchers lose traffic, and your tender court
Browse, like Assyria's king, on bloodless weeds;—
Ay, but our daggers shall be kept on edge,
To stab our kind! Well, you are happily matched:
A squeamish king who circumvents two lives,
To urge his purpose to its bloody end,
Vowing that justice shall have one of them,
And a meek queen who shudders at the means,
Yet at the end grapples with furies' claws.
You crocodiles can blubber o'er your prey,
If a stray infant should fall overboard,

And cry that drowning is a sorry thing,
Ere you together gorge it! What a life,
So comforting to conscience, you may lead
When Hymen yokes you!—Damn hypocrisy!

Enter THOMAS WYATT.

WYATT.

So say I too, under your grace's oath.

NORFOLK.

Ha! ha! Sir Poet, 'twas a pious oath.

WYATT.

Of sure fulfilment.

NORFOLK.

Pray what brings you here?

WYATT.

A moth to light, a poet to a prince;
Thus is it ever. I would see the king.

NORFOLK.

He just retired.

WYATT.

'Tis but a small affair;
I'll come again.

NORFOLK.

Can I not aid you, sir?

WYATT.

I merely wished to see a prisoned rogue—
One fellow Smeaton, caged for stealing geese,
Or some such matter. Has your grace a pass?
The careless knave had my last madrigal
To set for music. 'Tis my only copy;
And if he is hanged, my immortality
Loses a hope. Now, reynard, play the fool! (*Aside.*)

NORFOLK.

So ho! my railer at hypocrisy,
How smooth we lie! (*Aside.*) Confound this gosling thief!
The king has ordered—why I cannot say—
That none except the Council shall have leave
To see the fellow.

WYATT.

Well, there is little lost.

NORFOLK.

O much! O much! I honour poesy;
And vow to succour your brave madrigal.—
I'll make especial business of this matter.

WYATT.

As deep as hell! (*Aside.*) Nay, trouble not yourself;
Perchance the knave, among his prison·griefs,
Has lost remembrance of my trifling song.

NORFOLK.

I will refresh him. 'Twould amaze you, sir,
To know how much I reverence your art.
Each genuine poet, in each poem, forms
What neither he nor any other man,
Though he were equal in capacity,
Can shape again. The moods of poets' minds
Are, like the colours of chameleons,
Seen in the same particulars but once.
That combination of your shifting thoughts,
Which you have pictured in a madrigal,
Should make its due impression on our time.

I would not see your chaplet lose a leaf:—
Believe me, 'tis a duty.

WYATT.

Cunning hound,
With what a relish he pursues intrigues! (*Aside.*)
I thank your grace, in poesy's sweet name,
For this regard. Pray, can you tell me, sir,
Upon what charge my friend, Sir Henry Norris,
Will be arraigned?

NORFOLK.

On many, many, sir.
The gravest, I believe, is robbing goose-ponds:—
He is involved with Smeaton.

WYATT.

Ah! indeed?
'Tis an odd charge! But I observe of late
How our good king takes the most famous geese,
This realm produces, 'neath his royal wing.
Adieu! your grace. (*Going.*)

NORFOLK.

Ho! scion of the muse!
I have a little scandal for your ear.

WYATT.

For mine, your grace? (*Returns.*)

NORFOLK.

Yes; 'tis a trifling thing,—
No greater in my eyes than songs in yours.
They say you read too many madrigals
In the attentive hearing of the queen.
Look to it, sir: his majesty is loth
His royal consort should give up her time
To so much poetry.

WYATT.

The sneering cur!
I dare not brave him, for her highness' sake. (*Aside.*)
An idle rumour.

NORFOLK.

But it put your songs
In fearful jeopardy. The king nigh swore
To hang all future poems by the neck,
In your good person. He hates poesy.
The royal opposition on this point
Is stranger than the patronage of geese.

WYATT.

'Sblood! I must burst, if I remain to hear
This cynic's gibes. (*Aside.*) Farewell! once more.

NORFOLK.

Remembei,
No private readings to her majesty
Of the lost madrigal, when I restore it.

WYATT.

God shield the queen! for human aid is vain. (*Aside.*)
[*Exeunt severally.*

SCENE V.

The Queen's Apartments in the Palace. A table spread. QUEEN ANNE, MAIDS, *and* ATTENDANTS, *at the back of the scene.*

QUEEN ANNE. (*Advancing.*)

Ah me! what fearful difference 'tis, to view
The self-same object unattained and won!
For memories are the shadows of our hopes,

That ever lengthen as our day declines,
Till death's oblivion wraps them both in night.
When, from the lowly vale of common life,
Ambition points us to the sunny tops
Of the great hills of power, whose even sides,
Ascending smoothly through the golden haze,
Appear like stepping-stones from earth to heaven—
Ah! who could tell the peril of the road
That must be braved to reach their eminence?
What stony paths—what thorny barriers—
What humble crawling under threatening rocks—
What dizzy ledges, wooing nerveless fear
To swift forgetfulness—what hungry chasms,
That picture death within their roaring jaws,
And stagger reason on his solid throne—
Must be o'erpassed, ere on the toppling heights,
Amidst the region of perpetual storms,
We stand alone in chill supremacy!

Enter THOMAS WYATT.

Quick, Wyatt, quick! have my poor friends a hope?

WYATT.

But in the mercy of your enemies,
Or the most tardy justice of the king.

QUEEN ANNE.

Is this your zeal? O apathetic man!
Can you see Rochford, noble, loyal Rochford—
Your friend, your playmate—one who ever bore
His gathering honours with such humbleness
That my hot pride has chid him—can you see
George Boleyn pining in a dreary cell,
While May's warm sunshine fills the universe?
Bethink you, Wyatt, of those faithful men,
Weston, and Brereton, and Henry Norris,
Whose days, like fetters, gall their manly souls,
In the cramped limits of a prison house,
While you are slack to free them!

WYATT.

Gracious Heaven!—

QUEEN ANNE.

Deeds would be better, sir, than windy oaths.
Lend me your manhood for a little day,
And, by my soul, I'll breach their prison doors,
Or light a blaze in England that shall scare
These skulking enemies of theirs and mine
Into a frenzy! Heaven can testify,

How much it grieves me that their doleful fate
Seems woven with the tissue of my own!
For were it not, their wrongs would muster friends,
And Heaven would launch an angry squadron down,
To succour virtue such as they possess.
But I—oh God! I stand here all alone,
Shunned by mankind, and tossed by careless chance
To glut the appetite of enmity—
A helpless woman, full of wrongs and grief,
With nothing left me but the conscious power
By which the guiltless bear their martyrdom!

WYATT.

O woful day!

QUEEN ANNE.

Have you but vain regrets?

WYATT.

Hear me, your highness.

QUEEN ANNE.

Words, and nothing more.
Has innocence no power? has justice fled
The side of right? or is it mere romance,

To prate with poets of a heavenly might
That nerves the weakness of a righteous cause?
Fie! dreamer, fie!

WYATT.

I ask you not to laud
My wakeful labour, day and night bestowed,
Without a thought of safety for myself,
Upon this hopeless matter; all I ask,
Is thankless justice for a pure intent.
I grant my efforts were of no avail—
I grant some other and more skilful hand
Might have achieved a work beyond my power;
But O believe, all intellectual strength,
All hidden cunning, and all bold resource,
That nature gave me, were employed in vain
Ere I despaired.

QUEEN ANNE.

What was this mighty work?
Had you the labour of a Hercules,
That you so groan? Upon my life, I think
This wondrous malady will heal itself

Without your aid.—Shake not your solemn head.
The king still loves me:—I have faith in love.

WYATT.

Ha! have you faith? then see my very heart.
My memory reaches not that early day
When I first loved you. Since remembrance threw
The bright reflections of my childish thoughts
Into the gloom of manhood's troubled hours,
There is not a gleam, howe'er remote and dim,
But owes its splendour to my love for you;
There is not a hope—

QUEEN ANNE.

Hold, traitor, on your life!
Are you conspiring with my subtle foes?
My maids observe us.—Would you ruin me?
Is my last friend corrupted? Dare you, sir,
Prattle this nonsense to your queen? O base!
Thus to presume on my defencelessness;
Implying frailty which, a week ago,
You had better died than barely hinted at!

WYATT.

You thought me lukewarm.

QUEEN ANNE.

No; I only meant
To whet the edge of blunted zeal. (*Noise without.*)

WYATT.

How now?
Prophetic fear!

Enter Duke of NORFOLK, *Duke of* SUFFOLK, *and other Lords of the Council, with Sir* WILLIAM KINGSTON *and* GUARD.

QUEEN ANNE.

Good welcome, gentlemen!
Bear you a message from his majesty?

(*A long pause.*)

What, not a word?

SUFFOLK.

We do.

QUEEN ANNE.

Do what, your grace?

SUFFOLK.

Bear you a message from the king.

QUEEN ANNE.

Ha! ha! (*Laughing.*)
Your answer lagged so far behind my query,
As quite to rupture sense.

NORFOLK.

Come, Suffolk, come;
No faltering now. (*Apart to* SUFFOLK.)

SUFFOLK.

The king has ordered us,
To see the person of her majesty
Placed in your hands, Sir William, until he
Makes such disposure of her as may suit
His further pleasure.

QUEEN ANNE.

Back, ye urgent tears;
I'll never pay your tribute to my foes! (*Aside.*)
If 'tis the pleasure of his majesty
To change my present lodgings for the Tower,
Like a true subject, I obey.

WYATT.

Brave, brave!
Nature created thee from royal clay! (*Aside.*)

KINGSTON.

I will await your highness' preparation.

QUEEN ANNE.

I need none, sir.

NORFOLK.

Away, away, Sir William!

QUEEN ANNE.

Well said, good uncle. [*Exeunt all but* WYATT.

WYATT.

O were I a beast,
And Norfolk but another, I would tear
The bitter heart out of his spiteful breast!
But as a man—O, as a gentleman,
A Christian gentleman—I thank his grace
That he allows my littleness to crawl
'Neath God's own light, and fret my weary soul
With gazing on his huge monstrosity!
What next? what next?—Divorce! And then, poor queen,
She'll sit her down, like injured Katharine,
And feed her heart with sorrow, till the bane

Of cankering grief has poisoned every spring
That pulses life along her shattered frame;
And then she'll lapse, by scarce perceived degrees,
Into her grave; and then—why then the world
Will roar and scramble o'er her resting-place,
And play the same stale antics which she saw,
And dash its brimming tides of ruddy life
Across her tomb, without a care for her.—
O! should we laugh or weep at human fate?
There goes to shame the only mortal thing
I ever loved, with all a poet's love,
And I ask that, in mockery of myself! (*Weeps.*)

[*Scene closes.*

SCENE VI.

Before the gate of the Tower. Enter QUEEN ANNE, *in custody of Sir* WILLIAM KINGSTON *and* GUARD, *Duke of* NORFOLK, *Duke of* SUFFOLK, *and* LORDS *of the Council.*

QUEEN ANNE.

Pause here a moment.

NORFOLK.

Tut! tut! move along.

QUEEN ANNE.

Did you not, sir, insult your queen enough,
Before the Council, with unmanly taunts
And slanders, rivalled in their gross excess
But by the words in which you uttered them,
Without disgracing thus your victory?

NORFOLK.

It ill beseems my noted chastity
To hold discourse with ladies of your stamp.
Stop, if you list; I'd rather grant your wish
Than parley with you.

QUEEN ANNE.

Aid me, gracious Lord,
To bear unmurmuring! (*Aside.*) Listen, gentlemen.
'Tis the last time, perchance, that I may stand
Beneath the open blessings of the sky;
And here, before the majesty of heaven,
Gazing unshaken in the face of God,
I solemnly avow these horrid crimes,

With which my enemies have vested me,
To be most foul and baseless calumnies;—
Or God forsake me in my strictest need!

NORFOLK.

What monstrous perjury! I dare not hear
This woman's self-damnation. (*Going.*)

SUFFOLK.

Come, my lords;
Our part is done. [*Exit with* NORFOLK *and the Lords.*

QUEEN ANNE.

Their scorn foreshows my doom:
I am convicted ere the court be met.
Think you I shall have justice?

KINGSTON.

Without doubt:
The poorest subject of the king has that.

QUEEN ANNE.

Ha! ha! poor man! (*Laughing.*) Loyal credulity!
O yes, at last—in heaven. Where go I, sir?—
Into a dungeon?

KINGSTON.

No, your majesty;
You lie in the state chambers.

QUEEN ANNE.

In which rooms?

KINGSTON.

Where you were lodged on coronation day.

QUEEN ANNE.

This is too cruel!

KINGSTON.

Is splendour cruelty?

QUEEN ANNE.

O you are gracious! They are far too good
For such a wretch—so abject, so forlorn,
A prisoned felon;—were it not that they
Will taunt my memory with a pleasant dream,
That there once practised on my facile hopes,
While reason slept. Alas, alas, for me!
Time, like a mocking showman, turns the picture,
To teach on what coarse stuff my fancy wrought.

KINGSTON.

Time may relent, and make all well erelong.
Your slight constraint shall not seem bondage to you.

QUEEN ANNE.

It matters not, if we are prisoners,
Whether our walls be marked by feet or miles:
I may be cramped and tethered in my will,
While my clay roams the starry universe;—
What but free will is freedom?

KINGSTON.

Shall we enter?

QUEEN ANNE.

Your pardon, sir, if I have wearied you
With my complaints. But you have heard to-day
Things that might break a prouder heart than mine.
I do confess, my slanderers have wrought
More on my spirits than I once believed
Mere malice could.—Was it not vile?

KINGSTON.

Poor queen, poor queen! (*Aside.*) I cannot judge, your highness.

QUEEN ANNE.

I should not ask you to o'erstep discretion.
Where is the king?

KINGSTON.

At York Place, I believe.

QUEEN ANNE.

Will you convey his majesty a note?

KINGSTON.

I cannot.

QUEEN ANNE.

Cannot! but a message then?
Tell him—

KINGSTON.

Indeed I dare not.

QUEEN ANNE.

Then, good sir,
Pray bear a letter to the Chancellor.

KINGSTON.

I am prohibited.

QUEEN ANNE.

Are you a tool?

KINGSTON.

Ay, but a feeling one.

QUEEN ANNE.

Forgive me, pray!
O you are kind, most kind! My hasty spleen
Must be abated to my present state.
Come, let us in. I may be dull, perchance;
But, as I live, I cannot realize
That he, the father of my little child,
Could so far banish all regard for me
As to afflict me with deliberate wrong.
No, no; I have been schooled to fearful thoughts,
But this, this cannot enter. Come, set on!

[*Exeunt into the Tower.*

ACT V.

SCENE I. *A Room in Whitehall Palace.* KING HENRY *and* JANE SEYMOUR.

JANE SEYMOUR.

Nay, my sweet Henry, shrink not for a thought.
Wisdom is Janus-faced, and boldly looks
Not only at dead acts of bygone times,
But, in the very front of coming years,
Stands forth a prophet to foretell events.
Why should we dream upon the harmless past,
If not to shape the future of our lives
By its dear purchased knowledge?

KING HENRY.

True enough.

JANE SEYMOUR.

See then what follows. Should Queen Anne die,
And no male issue bless your majesty,

Elizabeth, your so-called daughter, reigns.—
So-called, I say; for where is your warranty
To deem her truer than her faithless dam?

KING HENRY.

Right, by my soul! I'll disinherit her;
My Parliament shall set her claim aside:
We'll have no bastards on our English throne,
To mock our justice.

JANE SEYMOUR.

Ah! the Parliament!
But what it does, it can undo again.

KING HENRY.

Ay, ay; 'twere safer to divorce the queen,
And so, as in our daughter Mary's case,
Cut off Elizabeth.

JANE SEYMOUR.

'Twill trouble you,
For many a weary day, if the bold queen
Should stand up stiffly for her royal rights,
Nor yield to you.

KING HENRY.

"Nor yield?"—'ods wounds! she shall!
I'll have each tittle of my liberty,
Ere we break quits. Why, it were monstrous, base,
To offer our good subjects her vile sprout
By way of queen! 'Twas rumoured, at her birth,
That Bess was not my own.

Enter Duke of NORFOLK.

In good time, Norfolk —
How proceeds our cause?

NORFOLK.

Slowly, my liege.

KING HENRY.

Push on, push on!

NORFOLK.

Ha, ha! my royal hound,
Do you scent blood at last? (*Aside.*) Mark Smeaton now
Will swear to anything beneath the moon;
But all the others are intractable.
When of their common guilt we question them,
Rochford but gives a melancholy smile;

Weston stares at us with his great bright eyes,
As if he doubted of our sanity;
Brereton, scowling, fumbles for his sword;
And Henry Norris has gone virtue-mad:
He raves and swears about his innocence,
And vows he never will accuse the queen,
Whom in his conscience he believes most pure.

KING HENRY.

Hang him up, hang him up then!

NORFOLK.

Wonderful!
He grows blood-thirsty. 'Twas but yesterday
He saved a fly from drowning; and so talked,
And moralized so sweetly on this theme,
As nigh re-drowned the insect in his tears. (*Aside.*)
Yes; but before he hangs, could we succeed
In throwing him, or one of gentle blood,
Into the balance 'gainst her majesty,
'Twould show her light as air.

JANE SEYMOUR.

You doubt her guilt?

NORFOLK.

Not I, my lady; but opinion weighs
No atom in the jealous scales of law.

KING HENRY.

We'll suit the triers to the evidence.
She is false, without debate; then wherefore, sir,
Should we be nice about the means we use?
A band of angels, sworn upon our side,
Could not increase her guilt.

NORFOLK.

Doubtless, my liege;
But 'twould convict her to the common mind:
For, as we stand, this base-born, wavering groom
Is our sole witness; and we lose respect
By such a tottering basis to our cause.
The people—

KING HENRY.

Furies seize them, root and branch!
Here comes that bugbear of a timid court,
That noisy nothing, to assail our ears!
Sir, I more reverence a flock of geese—

Being a Roman in that one idea—
Than all the banded folly of the earth.
Is there more wisdom in a million fools
Than one alone? Shall foolery gain respect
By bare addition?

JANE SEYMOUR.

Please your majesty,
His grace but cares for your committed honour
In this regard.

KING HENRY.

I know his loyalty:
But shall a monarch answer to a mob
For private deeds? Lord, save their silliness!
'Tis scarce a twelvemonth, since they howled at us
"We'll have no Nanny Boleyn for our queen!"
And now they saint her! Norfolk, look at them
As on a crowd of human weathercocks,
That ever point right in the teeth of power,
Howe'er it veer. Join me anon, your grace;
I fain would hit upon some speedy scheme
That may annul my marriage with the queen.
Sweetheart, come walk.

NORFOLK.

I will attend your highness.

[*Exeunt* KING HENRY *and* JANE SEYMOUR.

So all this pother, all this hanging men,
Divorcing wives, and chopping off one's head,
Is for mere happiness—an endless chase!
As if a man, so stuffed with memories
Of the dark path that led him to his hopes,
Could taste enjoyment if he reached his wish.
Good Lord, a king may be a royal fool!
This outdoes alchymy.—I had rather fight
'Gainst nature for the boon of endless life,
And hope to turn God's purpose upside down—
Chase the horizon till I found the spot
Where heaven meets earth, and, with that blissful kiss,
Rains joy celestial on the duller land—
Run down the rainbow to the golden spring
Of its bright arch—believe a poet's dream—
Do any shallow thing, but set sound wits
Upon a chase for phantom happiness.
Ha, ha! king motley! Give me power, power, power!

[*Exit slowly.*

SCENE II.

The State Apartments in the Tower. QUEEN ANNE *alone.*

QUEEN ANNE.

Ye rugged walls, how often have ye heard
The weary moans of prisoned innocence,
By bondage plundered of its cheerful spirit,
Broken in will, bankrupt in energy;
And when at last thought has so preyed on thought,
As to debase the judgment's faculty,
Robbed of that God-sustaining power of right
Which lifts the soul above calamity?
O wo! O wo! shall I become at length
A mental wreck, a chaos of despair,
With scarcely strength in my enervate mind
To see the conscience-drawn dividing line
That marks the boundary between right and wrong?
Alas! I fear it; for I cannot tell
What high prerogative, that once was mine,
I would not barter for mere liberty.

Enter, behind, LADY BOLEYN *and* MRS. COSYNS.

LADY BOLEYN.

Still lost in thoughts.

MRS. COSYNS.

I'll warrant them not good.

LADY BOLEYN.

Then stand aside. If she should utter aught,
Above a whisper, we can catch its sense.

MRS. COSYNS.

Then to his grace, and so unto the king.
Good luck! my lady, it is merry this,
To be familiar with their majesties—
To be the very spirit of the words
That go between them.

LADY BOLEYN.

Hush! the queen begins.

QUEEN ANNE.

This awful pause—this quivering of the beam
That balances my hesitating fate—
This watchful agony of rigid sense,

Bending all faculties in one fixed stare,
That hangs upon the dial of events,
And counts the passing moments, without power
To urge or slacken their relentless course—
Would make a faith in settled destiny
Far preferable to chance. Then stolid force
Might brazen out the frowns of hopeless fate,
And learn to suffer what it could not change.
But O the thought that we, the rulers born
Of time and fortune and opposed events,
Can be so meshed in outward circumstance,
As to lose influence o'er our very lives,
Gives to adversity its bitterest pangs,
And takes from will its living soul of hope.

LADY BOLEYN.

That's rare philosophy, I question not,
But it is bad religion.

MRS. COSYNS.

Terrible!

QUEEN ANNE.

Avenging Heaven, and I deserve it all!

LADY BOLEYN.

That's broad confession.

MRS. COSYNS.

Shameless! How she dared
The wrath of Heaven, in her stout impudence!

QUEEN ANNE.

Yes, I deserve it; but 'tis double pain,
To feel the chastisements of angry Heaven
Meted to me in seeming punishment
For that whereof I am guiltless.

LADY BOLEYN.

Heard you that?

MRS. COSYNS.

Nay, I am a little deaf.

QUEEN ANNE.

O Wolsey, Wolsey!
I, whose ambitious footstep thrust aside
Your tottering age—I, who with crafty toil
Climbed to the seat of patient Katharine—
Feel every pang with which I tortured you.

My power is gone; another cunning maid
Plays o'er my part of heartless treachery.
O More and Fisher—blood, blood!—save my wits!—
If fate like theirs should close my history,
To make Heaven's doom complete! Why shrink at that?
For 'tis but one, among a thousand ways,
Of stepping from the world. And what were life,
Declining by degrees of misery
To chill oblivion?—Queen of yesterday—
The rabble's pity—an old doting crone,
That some fool's grandsire, "Marry, knew as queen!"
Rattling her toothless jaws in silly prate
About herself—"And how they crowned her once,
With a great crown all full of shining stones;
And what brave velvet farthingales she wore;
And how she reigned; and, well-a-day, how fell!"
Pah! it sets death a-laughing. Gracious Heaven,
But grant my sinfulness one little prayer—
'Tis all I ask—drive on the lagging days,
And bring this matter to its fated end;
For there are seeds of madness in my grief
That must o'ertop my reason!

Lady Boleyn *and* Mrs. Cosyns *advance.*

MRS. COSYNS.

Please you, lady.
(*To* Queen Anne.)

LADY BOLEYN.

Your majesty.

MRS. COSYNS.

She hears us not.

QUEEN ANNE.

Well, well!
But Rochford, ay, and all my noble friends,
Crowded together in a general doom;
As if mine enemies had sworn to leave
No vestige of me. Bitter, bitter hate!
My father next—

MRS. COSYNS.

Yes, please you, he is well.

QUEEN ANNE.

Who spoke?

MRS. COSYNS.

Your servant.

QUEEN ANNE.

Service without love.

LADY BOLEYN.

You wrong her much.

QUEEN ANNE.

You too, false kinswoman?

LADY BOLEYN.

Marry, and if your highness had not held
Such high opinion of familiar friends,
You had ne'er been here. 'Tis a good worldly rule,
As treachery harms more than enmity,
To tell no tales but what we tell our foes.

QUEEN ANNE.

Deep in the world, but shallow in the heart.
What brings you here?

LADY BOLEYN.

The welfare of yourself,
And the deliverance of your noble brother,
With all his prisoned friends.

QUEEN ANNE.

When owls can sing,
I'll listen, cousin.

LADY BOLEYN.

Scold, but credit me.

QUEEN ANNE.

What is the price? If it involve my life,
I'll coin my heart's blood, to the utmost drop,
But I will pay it.

LADY BOLEYN.

'Tis that you agree
To offer no obstruction to the king
In his proposed divorce.

QUEEN ANNE.

Dare you insult—
Nay, nay, forgive my haste. Is it the king
Who wills his daughter's shame? who barters life
On terms that blacken mercy's reverend hand,
And sink her calling to mere brokery?
Is this divorce his wish?

MRS. COSYNS.

It is, your highness;
I had it from his lips.

LADY BOLEYN.

'Twill but oppose,
And not defeat his plan, if you refuse.
Denial carries death to all; when you,
By bare concession, gain a pregnant hope.

QUEEN ANNE.

Hope, hope for me! O God, what mockery!—
I wish for nothing. Show me, beyond doubt,
That 'tis the king's command, and I will yield.

MRS. COSYNS.

A wise conclusion.

QUEEN ANNE.

Spare your comments, madam:
My duty tutors better than your tongue.
The very vileness of this proffered trade
Gives it the lie. O 'tis far past belief,
To deem a father so unnatural:
Sure 'tis but trial of my patient love

The king intends.—Why, glimmering hopes seem born
From the sheer blackness of surrounding things,
Like little stars at midnight. (*Aside.*)

MRS. COSYNS.

Bless my soul,
Her highness smiles!

QUEEN ANNE.

Why not?

LADY BOLEYN.

Be still, you fool!
Her subtle mind is twisting in a net
Of its own flimsy thoughts. (*Apart to* MRS. COSYNS.)

MRS. COSYNS.

I am not your wench!
What the king orders me, I will perform,
Though all the Lady Boleyns in the land
Cry "Fool, and fool!" (*Apart to* LADY BOLEYN.)
If it would please your highness,
Now, while this candid mood possesses you,
To make confession to us of the crimes
For which you suffer; and so spare the king—

LADY BOLEYN.

The loose-tongued idiot! (*Aside.*)

QUEEN ANNE.

Out! you base-born wretch!
Are you a woman? Have you borne a child?
And would you snatch it from your wolfish breast,
To stamp the bastard on its baby brow?

MRS. COSYNS.

I have no child.

QUEEN ANNE.

Heaven keep you barren then,
You shameless slanderer of your mother's sex!
Dare you to traffic for my chastity—
The natural patent of all womanhood—
That more becomes my naked innocence
Than the great ring of jewelled royalty?
O, had I lost it, I would barter crown,
And queenly dignity—yea, life itself—
To wear it but one hour of agony,
Then hand it spotless to posterity.
Fie! you are rank, if you have never felt
Your sex's instinct!

MRS. COSYNS.

Lady, let us go:
Her majesty so storms—

LADY BOLEYN.

Yes, slink away,
You wretched marplot! (*Apart to* MRS. COSYNS.)

QUEEN ANNE.

Get to your prayers—go!
Send to your heart each drop of modest blood
That ever mustered in your virgin cheeks,
At wanton thoughts, to wash away this shame!

MRS. COSYNS.

Come, come; she'll rail again.
[*Exit with* LADY BOLEYN.

QUEEN ANNE.

This killing doubt!
What can it mean?—where am I?—is it real?
For I have read, how some have seemingly
Passed ages in a dream; have died and risen;
Have wandered on through shadows limitless,
And passed the radiant gates of Paradise,

To dwell for days unnumbered with the Saints;
Have woke at last, and found the blazing sun,
That shaped the fancies of their lengthened vision,
Just peeping from the east. Is life a dream?
Is time a mere illusion of the mind?
And shall we waken from our restless sleep,
To see the glory-beaming face of God
Smile in our eyes a summons to that life
Where all is real? What to my endless soul
Is this flat pageantry of days and years?
Events, not hours, are measurers of our lives,
And I in deeds have far outlived my term;
While sorrows, heavier than three score and ten
May often totter under, bow my head,
That only needs the hoary badge of time
To make old age complete. Why should I stand
And dally thus with my kind landlord, death,
Upon the threshold of his narrow house,
While all without is dark and shelterless,
And all so bright within? Why fear to leave
The fickle favours that mankind bestow,
For the sure bounties of Omnipotence?
O God, I know not! but my startled heart

Rises in loud rebellion at the hint
Of that chill power whose torpid tyranny
Shall still its play forever. Love, fame, power—
Ay, all, all, everything, the uttermost!—
Have vanished in the shadow of my wrongs;
And yet I gripe life's load of misery,
As if there were a hope beyond my loss! [*Exit.*

SCENE III.

The Gate of the Tower, surrounded by a crowd of Citizens, endeavouring to enter, who are kept back by a guard of men-at-arms. Enter, from the Tower, FIRST CITIZEN.

CITIZENS.

What news, what news?

FIRST CITIZEN.

What news can you expect?

SECOND CITIZEN.

The queen's deliverance.

FIRST CITIZEN.

Nonsense! where the king
Is chief accuser?

THIRD CITIZEN.

Ay; but justice, sir.

FIRST CITIZEN.

Speak not so loud; the lords might overhear,
And lose their loyalty.

THIRD CITIZEN.

What mean you, friend?

FIRST CITIZEN.

Her highness is prejudged, and, save in form,
Doomed ere her cause be heard.

SECOND CITIZEN.

Made she defence?

FIRST CITIZEN.

O yes, most eloquent and strongly knit:
Beauty and truth came hand in hand together,
To breathe their essence in each modest word.—
But what avails an angel's purity

Where devils judge? 'Tis a bare legal form,
This solemn meeting of her enemies,
Disguising hate in ermined justice' gown.

SECOND CITIZEN.

This is blunt talk.

FIRST CITIZEN.

But true.

THIRD CITIZEN.

But dangerous,
To speak and hear.

FIRST CITIZEN.

What are state trials now,
More than the whetting of the headsman's axe?
We English people have forgot the rights
Which God and nature give to every man:
Our common justice is a common drab—
A pliant doxy, openly deboshed—
That winks beneath her twisted blind at lords,
Doffs it for kings—

CITIZENS.

Forbear, forbear!

FIRST CITIZEN.

Pshaw, sirs!
I am a careless, melancholy man,
Who would not change a notion for my life.
I sought this trial of her majesty
To escape myself for a brief interval;
But, as I live, it crowded in such thoughts
Upon my proper griefs, that I had rather
Be damned to wear the memory of a fiend,
Than witness such another.

THIRD CITIZEN.

Friends, away!
This man is vile, upon his own confession.
Lord, sirs, what words were these!

FIRST CITIZEN.

Slink, cowards, slink!
Get to your slavish homes! Brush up your caps!
Practise your loyal lungs! Make ready all
To startle Heaven, when good Queen Anne dies,
With "God preserve Queen Jane!"

THIRD CITIZEN.

This man is mad.

SECOND CITIZEN.

Nay, sirs, but simple.

FIRST CITIZEN.

O that all of you,
Two-legged crawlers to ignoble graves,
Were half so mad as I! [*Exit.*

THIRD CITIZEN.

Poor soul, poor soul!
Where is his keeper? He may come to harm.

SECOND CITIZEN.

Let us take the fool's advice, and hurry home;
For there's no chance of entrance to the Tower.

[*Exeunt.*

SCENE IV.

The Great Hall of the Tower, arranged for the Queen's trial. On one side are seated Dukes of NORFOLK, SUFFOLK, *and* RICHMOND, *Marquis of* EXETER, *Earl of* ARUNDEL, *and other Peers, as Lords Triers, with Officers, &c.; on the other,* QUEEN ANNE, *in the custody of Sir* WILLIAM KINGSTON, *Ladies, Attendants, Guards, &c.*

NORFOLK.

Are we agreed? (*To the Lords.*)

SUFFOLK.

Here is our verdict, sir.

(*Hands a paper.*)

(RICHMOND *and* SUFFOLK *talk apart.*)

RICHMOND.

I hope, your grace, I have damned my soul enough
To please the most fastidious father.

SUFFOLK.

Stuff!

RICHMOND.

Yes, "stuff!" substantial, downright villany,
That I shall bear upon my aching heart
Till death unload it.

SUFFOLK.

Come, be cheerful, sir.
It ill becomes heroic minds to shrink
From the first blood of triumph. You are young,
And dainty-minded; time will strengthen you.

RICHMOND.

Courage but adds deformity to crime.
A wicked heart, though placid in the girth
Of stern control, which rigid will upheaves,
Can but reflect each blessing of sweet heaven,
And every bordering virtue of our earth,
All topsyturvy. I am hardened, sir;
If not by years, at least by sinfulness—
That wrinkled register of ill-spent days—
Who scars his moments on the erring heart
While yet the brow is smooth.

SUFFOLK.

The saints look down!

This pretty sermon must have washed you clean.
Hist! hear the sentence.

NORFOLK.

Lady Anne Boleyn,
Marchioness of Pembroke, sometime England's queen—
Though most unworthily, as the strict course
Of equal justice has so clearly proved—
Arise. (*The* QUEEN *rises.*) Lay off your crown and vestured marks
Of royal dignity, to hear from me
The solemn finding of this high tribunal.

(QUEEN ANNE *puts off her crown and robe of state.*)

QUEEN ANNE.

Your grace's first commands, though harshly meant,
Are merciful indeed.

NORFOLK.

Be silent, madam!
Upon each several charge, whereon you stand
Indicted by the law, we do pronounce
Your guilt most clear; and therefore do condemn you,
At such time as his majesty may name,

To suffer death by burning at the stake,
Or by beheading, as may please the king.—
God give you patience to endure your doom!

QUEEN ANNE.

I doubt it not. O Father, O Creator,
Who art the way, the life, the truth, Thou know'st
If I deserve this death!

RICHMOND.

O base, base, base!
This pardons Herod in the eye of Heaven. (*Aside.*)

NORFOLK.

Marchioness of Pembroke, have you aught to say
Touching the judgment of this court?

QUEEN ANNE.

My lords,
I will not say your sentence is unjust,
Presuming that my reasons can prevail
Against your firm convictions, I had rather
Believe that you have reasons for your acts,
Of ample power to vindicate your fames;
But then they must be other than the court

Has heard produced: for by the evidence
I have been cleared, to all unbiassed minds,
Of each offence 'gainst which that proof was brought.
I have been ever to his majesty
A faithful wife: O could I say as truly,
That I have shown him the humility
His goodness, and the honour he conferred,
Deserved from me! I have, I do confess,
Had jealous fancies and suspicious thoughts—
In which, perchance, I wronged him—that had I
Been more discreet and anxious to conceal,
I had been more the queen, but less the wife.
God is my witness, that in no way else
Have I e'er sinned against him.
Think not, my lords, I say this to prolong
My heavy life; for God has fortified
My trust in Him, and taught me how to die.
Think me not so bewildered in my mind,
As not to lay my chastity to heart,
Now in my last extremity; for I
Have held its honour far above my crown,
And have maintained no queenly dignity
More pure from vulgar stain. I know my words

Can naught avail me, save to justify
My chastity, so periled by your doom.
As for my brother, and those constant friends
With me unjustly sentenced, I would die
A thousand deaths to save their guiltless lives:
But since it has so pleased his majesty,
I will accompany them, most willingly,
Through death to heaven, through pain to endless peace.
I have said all.

NORFOLK.

Remove the prisoner.

[QUEEN ANNE *bows to the Court, and is led off by Sir* WILLIAM KINGSTON. *Then exeunt all but the Lords Triers.*

RICHMOND.

We are damned forever!

NORFOLK.

Poh, poh! saved, I think.
While she held power heads flew like tennis-balls.

ARUNDEL.

Why did she touch so lightly on the king?

EXETER.

'Twas for a cause no deeper than the heart,—
She loves him yet.

ARUNDEL.

The sentimental fool!

NORFOLK.

Would you wrong women, and yet have them blind
To every injury you dare conceive?—
Get them to love you.

EXETER.

Ah! your grace, I fear
He'll ne'er wrong woman.

NORFOLK.

Gentlemen, away!
Our sun of power is burning in mid air;
We waste the daylight. Come, let us seek the king.
Hug every Seymour that you chance to meet! [*Exeunt.*

SCENE V.

The State Apartments in the Tower. QUEEN ANNE *alone.*

QUEEN ANNE.

There is not a pang remains; there is not a wound,
That hate can give, at which my nerveless heart
Would shrink appalled. The storm of life has blown,
And rent my prospect into countless shreds,
Chaotic, undistinguished, featureless—
Without a point, before me or behind,
On which a once familiar eye may rest—
And all is calm again. Calm, very calm,—
An utter desolation fixed and grim,
And barren as the sand. No queen, no wife—
Ebbed to the lowest. O Elizabeth,
My helpless child, whose rights were all in me,
How could a mother blast her memory,
Even in thine eyes, by yielding to her foes
Thy royal heritage? Thou'lt hate me, love;
Thou'lt say thy mother wronged thee, eking out

Her worthless life with treasures stolen from thee;
Unweeting how thy uncle and my friends
Owed life to thee. Why must I wander down
All coming time to pick new sorrows out?—

(*A bell tolls.* QUEEN ANNE *rushes to the door.*)

Whose knell is that?

SENTINEL. (*Without.*)

Lord Rochford's.

QUEEN ANNE.

Duped, duped, duped!
O God! my brother!—Is there such a one
As an avenging God to look on this,
And not launch fire like rain? O shameless men!—
Men with God's raiment on their placid limbs—
Who almost swore his life should be preserved,
If I opposed not this divorce. O nature!—
Thou who dost send the harmless race of flowers,
And dews, and sunshine, and all gracious things—
What creatures hast thou sent to people earth,
And blot thy fair creation? Cut them down!
Or make this globe a dusty wilderness,
Fit for their habitation! Man, O man!

Thou art the only thing in nature's scheme
That seems disjointed from the harmony,—
The latest thought and worst!

Enter MARY WYATT.

MARY WYATT.

Your majesty—

QUEEN ANNE.

I prithee mock me not. I am no queen,
Nor wife, nor maid—I know not what I am!

MARY WYATT.

What has disturbed you?

QUEEN ANNE.

Did you hear that bell?

MARY WYATT.

Pray, pray forgive me! (*Kneels, weeping.*)

QUEEN ANNE.

Nay, I'll kneel to you,
If I have vexed you. (*A distant shot is heard.*)

Rochford! (*Another shot.*)
Norris! (*Another shot.*)
Weston! (*Another shot.*)
And Brereton! Why stop your cannon? Shoot!—
Shoot on, till half the world shall suffer death;
For you have slain the noblest part! No, no;
The next shall be my own!

MARY WYATT.

Alas! alas! (*Weeping.*)

QUEEN ANNE.

Why weep you, girl? My brother was in heaven,
Ere you could hear the noisy cannon-shot
Tell his departure.

MARY WYATT.

Would your highness fly,
If I could ope these hideous prison doors?

QUEEN ANNE.

Not for the world.

MARY WYATT.

My brother has a plan
To raise the common people in revolt—

QUEEN ANNE.

Hold, if you'd live! I yet am so much queen
As to protect my realm from traitor's arts.
How dare you plot these treasonable designs
Against the safety of his majesty?
Name it again, and, as I live, the king
Shall know your thoughts.

MARY WYATT.

'Twas but our love for you—

QUEEN ANNE.

How! love for me, and plotting 'gainst the king!

MARY WYATT.

Strange, very strange! (*Aside.*)

Enter Sir WILLIAM KINGSTON *and* GUARD.

QUEEN ANNE.

My time has come, Sir William?

KINGSTON.

It has, my lady.

QUEEN ANNE.

You delayed my death:

I should have died some hours ago. 'Tis cruel
To dally with my life.

KINGSTON.

'Twas not my fault.
The Council feared a rising of the commons,
And therefore changed the hour.

QUEEN ANNE.

Ha! ha! how weak!
(*Laughing.*)
Who cares about my death? Is Smeaton dead?

KINGSTON.

He is.

QUEEN ANNE.

And made he no amends to me?
Did he not own his monstrous perjuries?

KINGSTON.

Not that I heard.

QUEEN ANNE.

The impious, heartless wretch!

To dare o'erleap the doubtful gulf of death,
With such a fearful load!

MARY WYATT.

His death was just,
Even had he done no wrong,—the inborn felon!

QUEEN ANNE.

Nay, Mary, chide no more. Alas! poor Mark,
I fear thy soul is suffering for thy tongue.
Can I not see my daughter?

KINGSTON.

'Tis forbid.

QUEEN ANNE.

Well, I suppose the human frame can bear
More than I suffer—very little more.

KINGSTON.

My lady. (*Bell tolls.*)

QUEEN ANNE.

That speaks plainer, sir. I am ready.
I hope 'twill be but death, not butchery.

KINGSTON.

The pain is short.

QUEEN ANNE.

They call the headsman skilled;
And I—ha! ha!—see, good Sir William, see—
(*Laughing.*)
I have a little neck! (*Clasps her neck.*)

KINGSTON.

Why, is she mad?
I in my time have seen full many die,
But ne'er before saw one who laughed outright
At the mere thought of death. (*Aside.*)

(*Bell tolls.*)

QUEEN ANNE.

Come, Mary, come:
We keep death waiting.

MARY WYATT.

Heaven preserve her mind!
(*Aside.*)

QUEEN ANNE.

Set on, Sir William. You shall see, erelong,

How, like a bride, I'll meet this ugly death,
And make a triumph of my funeral!
Pray tell his majesty, in my behalf,
How much I thank him for his many favours.
He from a lady made me marchioness;
And from a marchioness he raised me up
To the full top of earthly power, a queen;
And last, his graces overrunning life,
He crowns my innocence with martyrdom.
My name is set above the reach of time,
A mark for men to carp and wonder at;
And some hereafter will believe me false,
Some think me true; bear witness, sir,
That with my latest breath I still declare
My perfect purity. (*Bell tolls.*) Set on, set on!

[*Exeunt.*

SCENE VI.

The Tower-Green. At the back of the stage is a scaffold, hung with black, on which are the block, Headsman, Attendants, Guard, &c. The Citizens gradually assemble in front of the scaffold. A bell tolls at long intervals.

FIRST CITIZEN.

I'll watch all day, but what I'll see her die.—
Let them change hours, I care not. Come along.

SECOND CITIZEN.

Here's a good stand.

THIRD CITIZEN.

Yes; if 'tis good to stand
And see our poor queen mangled.

FIRST CITIZEN.

"Poor queen," sooth!

SECOND CITIZEN.

You are a scholar, neighbour Marmaduke;

I pray you, was there e'er a queen before
Who graced a scaffold?

THIRD CITIZEN.

Ne'er before in England
Did monarch dare so try his people's patience.

FIRST CITIZEN.

We are in luck.

THIRD CITIZEN.

Fie! fie! you bloody knave!

FIRST CITIZEN.

Marry, and if a king cannot behead
His own liege wife, whom can he?

THIRD CITIZEN.

Monstrous dolt!

FIRST CITIZEN.

What were the good of treason then, if we
Could have no executions?—Mistress Maud,—
Hey! hey! you brought the children? (*To a woman.*)

WOMAN.

Yes indeed;
They cannot see a queen die every day.

THIRD CITIZEN.

You tiger-hearted woman, do you love
The sight of blood?

WOMAN.

Nay; the example, sir.

THIRD CITIZEN.

Lord! Lord! who ever caught a woman yet
Without pretexts in thousands!

FIRST CITIZEN.

'Tis a shame
To keep us honest people waiting so.

CITIZENS. (*Without.*)

The queen! the queen!

FIRST CITIZEN.

Move nearer.

CITIZENS.

Make way there!

Solemn music. Enter Duke of NORFOLK, *Duke of* SUFFOLK, *and other Noblemen;* QUEEN ANNE, *in custody of Sir* WILLIAM KINGSTON; MARY WYATT, *and other Maids of Honour; Guards, Attendants, &c. They mount the scaffold. Then enter, below,* THOMAS WYATT.

WYATT.

One look, no more. O wondrous, wondrous fair!
Death has made treaty with thy loveliness,
To hide the horrors that invest his state.
These spiteful clouds of earth-born misery
But add a glory to thy going down.
Slander, disgrace, fraud, legal infamy,
Imprisonment, this hideous form of death,
Each gains a splendour from its touch of thee
That robs regret of tears. How bright, how calm!
There is a voiceless sermon in that face,
To cheer the lonely heart of martyrdom,
And make it court its fate. O Anne, Anne!
The world may banish all regard for thee,
Mewing thy fame in frigid chronicles,
But every memory that haunts my mind
Shall cluster round thee still. I'll hide thy name

Under the coverture of even lines,
I'll hint it darkly in familiar songs,
I'll mix each melancholy thought of thee
Through all my numbers: so that heedless men
Shall hold my love for thee within their hearts,
Not knowing of the treasure. 'Twould be sin
To keep so fair a flower from paradise,—
That, in the very flush of earthly bloom,
Felt mildew blown on every ruffian wind,
And canker at the heart. Go, go,—farewell!
The sun that seems departing, to our eyes,
Is but arising on another land;
Thy death to us, is the short, painful birth
That ushers in thy taintless soul to heaven.—
Go, go! I would not raise a hand to keep thee here.

[*Exit.*

THIRD CITIZEN.

Be silent! Hear her majesty.

CITIZENS.

Hush, hush!

QUEEN ANNE.

Good Christian people, I am come to die,

According to the judgment of the law;
And therefore it would ill become me now,
After my doom is past, to censure it.
I am come hither to accuse no man,
Nor to say aught upon the many things
Whereof I am accused: for well I know
That my defence doth not pertain to you,
Nor from your favour could I hope for grace.
I am come here to die, to yield myself
To the king's will, with all humility.
I pray God save him, and extend his reign;
For he has been a gracious prince to you:
To me—I doubt not but his goodness went
Beyond my slender merit. I but ask,
Should you hereafter judge my luckless cause,
The best of each man's judgment. Now, farewell,
To you and to the world! Forget me not,
In the still places of your earnest prayers.
Attend me, maidens.

MARY WYATT.

Oh! not yet, not yet! (*Weeping.*)

QUEEN ANNE.

Well, I have played the waiting-maid before,
In happier hours. Alas! poor head, thou'lt roll
In a brief time amid this scaffold's dust;
As thou in life didst not deserve a crown,
So by thy doom is justice satisfied,
And her great beam repoised.

(Removing her collar and coifs.)

And ye, my damsels,
Who whilst I lived did ever show yourselves
So diligent in service, and are now
To be here present in my latest hour
Of mortal agony,—as in good times
Ye were most trustworthy, even so in this,
My miserable death, ye leave me not.
As a poor recompense for your rich love,
I pray you to take comfort for my loss—
And yet forget me not. To the king's grace,
And to the happier one whom you may serve
In place of me, be faithful as to me.
Learn from this scene, the triumph of my fate,
To hold your honours far above your lives.
When you are praying to the martyred Christ,

Remember me who, as my weakness could,
Faltered afar behind His shining steps,
And died for truth, forgiving all mankind.
The Lord have pity on my helpless soul!

(*Kneels at the block.*)

As the curtain falls, a peal of ordnance announces the death of QUEEN ANNE.

THE END.

www.ingramcontent.com/pod-product-compliance
Lightning Source LLC
LaVergne TN
LVHW011203110826
845150LV00006B/1307

* 9 7 8 1 4 2 5 5 1 8 4 6 2 *